AUTHENTIC THAI CUISINE

THAI

KITCHEN

Cookbook

Recipe development by:

Alexandra Eisler
Barbara B. Gray
Seth Jacobson
Peter Moore
Ernest W. Wong

Editor:
Cynthia Lawrence

Epicurean International, Inc,
Oakland, California USA

ISBN 0-9674895-0-4

Printed in Bangkok, Thailand.

Published and distributed by:
Thai Kitchen / Epicurean International, Inc.
229 Castro Street
Oakland, California 94607 USA
1.800.967.8424 (THAI)
PH. 510.268.0209
FAX 510.834.3102

e-mail: info@thaikitchen.com
http://www.thaikitchen.com

First Edition, 2000

Dedicated to the people of Thailand.

Introduction

Thailand has a lifestyle the rest of the world could envy. An independent nation founded in 1238, its original name, *Sukhothai*, means "Dawn of Happiness." Ever since, the Thai culture and cuisine have been based on pleasure and harmony.

Its neighbors, China, Laos, Cambodia, Burma, and India, have all contributed to Thailand's varied and zestful cuisine. However, Thai cooking has a character of its own, much of it based on the land's abundant spices and herbs.

Chili peppers in dozens of varieties give Thai cooking a reputation for being firecracker hot, but they are just one ingredient in the harmonious whole. Contrast and balance are what make a Thai meal: hot and spicy, sweet and sour, pungent and fragrant.

Brilliant taste, texture and color come from the fresh vegetables and fruits, the rich combinations of flavorings such as chilies, garlic and onions, curry mixtures, coriander, coconut cream, basil, lemon grass, mint, kaffir lime, and tamarind. Thailand's unique sauces add their own tang and may also be mixed into a dish to moderate its hotness. The most commonly found is fish sauce, its deliciously salty flavor used to season almost everything but sweets.

While Thais are not vegetarians -- and the barbecue dishes are marvelous -- meat and poultry are often used in small portions, almost as garnish, with emphasis on fruits and vegetables, fish and seafood. This is low-fat cuisine that seduces the senses, yet is packed with nutritional value.

In a country about the size of France, Thailand has a tropical climate and distinct regions. Each is as different from the others as the Rockies are to Florida. There are steamy jungles in Thailand's South, home to Indian-inspired curries and freshwater fish. Robust grilled meats and fiery sauces are native to the mountainous North. Orchards and vast rice paddies cover the fertile Central Plain. The long coastline of the Gulf Coast is famous for its white sands and bountiful fish and seafood. Bangkok is the cosmopolitan center of the nation, and every regional variation of Thai food can be found in its food stalls, cafes and elegant restaurants.

Much of the mystique surrounding Thai cuisine comes from the long tradition of elaborate food preparation known as palace cuisine. Intricate dishes are presented with garnishes of flowers and masterfully carved vegetables and fruits. In centuries past, not only did artisans become accomplished in palace cuisine decoration, as they still do today, it was not unusual for young ladies from royal or aristocratic families to study it as a household art form.

The other side of Thai cuisine is traditional home cooking. This is simple, hearty and flavorful. It can be a single dish, Western-style, or a Thai-style meal of several dishes to be enjoyed in the company of others.

Eating, Thai-Style

Thai Kitchen invites you to our table for a harmonious meal. Everything is set out at once, in no particular order, so you can fill your plate with a glorious variety of dishes. In the center of the table is a large bowl of steamed rice. Around it, you may find a soup, a curry, a stir-fry, a steamed dish, a salad, a sauce or two, fresh tropical fruit or a custard for dessert. The usual beverages are water, tea and fresh fruit juices.

Evening is when Thais eat the main meal of the day. Breakfast and lunch are light, possibly a snack or a single noodle dish. That's when you'd use your chopsticks, a custom inherited from the Chinese and their love of noodles. Otherwise, Thais eat mostly from a large spoon, using a fork to transfer tidbits of food onto the spoon.

Like any center of commerce today, life in Bangkok and the larger towns is speeded up. Family meals have fewer courses -- perhaps an easy stir-fry, the essential rice, a salad or vegetable, and fruit -- and meal preparation uses shortcuts. The complex sauces and dressings may be bottled, no longer from scratch, but the traditions of flavor and freshness remain strong. With a little chopping and stirring, who needs something frozen and zapped in the microwave!

Cooking, Thai-Style

Most Thai cooking is done in the wok, although a large skillet will do to get you started. This is simple and fast cooking, a technique of speedy hand movements that toss, stir and stir-fry. Just a little cooking oil or liquid is plenty. Ingredients are stirred and folded, with only brief contact with the high heat. Vegetables cooked this way for only a few seconds stay crisp and keep their bright colors. Stir-fries should be served immediately.

Many of the soups, stews and curries can be prepared up to a certain point in advance, then reheated and finished. If you don't want to make warm desserts at the last minute, cook them ahead, refrigerate, then serve at room temperature.

You won't need fancy equipment to show off your Thai cooking style. Here are your basics, most of which you may already own.

- Chopping block with a cleaver or large chef's knife
- Small paring knife
- Mortar and pestle for crushing garlic and spices
- Wok or large skillet
- Wok shovel or pancake turner for pushing and tossing food
- One or two large saucepans, or an electric steamer, for cooking rice

The key to effortless Thai cooking is advance preparation. Have all of your vegetables and meats chopped, cut or cubed. Line up your spices and sauces. The last thing you want when your guests are at the table, ready to admire your wok showmanship, is to have to stop and crush the garlic!

Use our recipes with enjoyment, and may happiness dawn at your own Thai table.

Our Menu Suggestions

Everyone's Favorite Thai Meal
Chicken, Pork, or Beef Satay
Hot & Sour Soup or Coconut Ginger Soup
Sweet Crispy Rice Noodles *(Mee Krob)*
Pad Thai Noodles
Green Curry with Basil *(Keow Wan Gai)*
Jasmine Rice
Sticky Rice with Coconut & Mango

The Perfect Cocktail Party
(All or a few of the following – depending on your number of guests)
Chicken, Pork, or Beef Satay
Veggie Kabobs or Eggplant Satay
Crab & Shiitake Spring Rolls
Shrimp, Proscuitto & Papaya Spring Rolls
Crispy Fish Cakes
Calamari Salad
Crispy Fried Tofu
Thai Barbecued Chicken Pizza
Bangkok Wings
Thai Barbecue Spareribs
Spicy Thai Pumpkin Nuts
Thai Barbecue Prawns or Garlic Shrimp
with
Thai Table Sauce
Cucumber Relish
Spicy Cucumber Sauce
Fiery Thai Salsa
Vegetable Dip

Quick Winter Meal
Hot & Sour Soup
Hot & Sour Pork Salad
Wide Noodles with Gravy & Broccoli *(Lad Nah)*

Appetizer Dinner
Crispy Fish Cakes
Sweet Pork
Spicy Clams with Basil
Lemon Grass Splash Beef Salad
Jasmine Rice

Tri-Salad Lunch
Thai Cobb Salad
Thai Rice Salad
Shrimp & Papaya Salad
Thai Iced Tea

Special Dinner Guests Menu
Bangkok Seafood Cocktail
Tom Yum Carrot Soup
Roast Duck Curry
Deep Fried Whole Fish
Stuffed Squid with Shiitake Mushroom Sauce
Jasmine Rice
Thai Coconut Pudding

Beautiful Presentation Meal
Sweet Crispy Rice Noodles *(Mee Krob)*
Spicy Clams with Basil
Stuffed Crab Shells
Coconut Baked in a Pumpkin
Sticky Rice with Coconut & Mango

Quick Lunch
Crispy Fish Cakes
Pad Thai Noodles
Thai Iced Tea

Vegetarian Dinner
Thai Squash Soup
Roasted Eggplant with Tofu and Basil
Wide Noodles with Gravy and Broccoli *(Lad Nah)*
Bangkok Fruit Salad

Outdoor Brunch for Two
Lemon Grass Splash Beef Salad
Peanut Noodles
Thai Summer Breeze
Coconut Corn Pudding

Quick Dinner
Thai Fried Rice
Spicy Broccoli
Green Curry Beef
Jasmine Rice

Thai Breakfast
Breakfast Rice Soup
Basic Thai Fried Rice
Thai Banana Smoothie

Sunday Night Family Dinner
Bangkok Wings
Sweet & Sour Tofu Stir-Fry
Tom Yum Corn Curry
Jasmine Rice
Peanut Noodles
Fresh Melon Slices

Easy Family Supper
Mixed Greens with Lemon Grass Salad Splash
BBQ Garlic Chicken
Veggie Kabobs
Jasmine Rice
Coconut Corn Pudding

Shore Dinner
Sour Prawn Soup
Steamed Salmon with Thai Herbs
Spicy Broccoli
Red Curry Shrimp
Thai Bananas in Coconut Milk

Casual Get Together with Friends
Thai Gazpacho served in Mugs
Barbecued Chicken Pizza
Sweet Pork
Spicy Corn Salad
Coconut Custard Baked in a Pumpkin

The Comfort Meal
Masuman Beef Stew
Green Curry with Vegetables *(Keow Wan)*
Jasmine Rice
Thai Tapioca Pudding

Barbecue. Thai-Style
(All or a few of the following – depending on your number of guests)
Chicken, Pork or Beef Satay
Roast Chili Flank Steak
Pork Loin with Chili Sauce *(Kaw Moo Yang)*
Herb-Grilled Chicken with Thai BBQ Sauce
BBQ Garlic Chicken
Veggie Kabobs
Jasmine Rice

The Fusion Meal
Shrimp, Proscuitto & Papaya Spring Rolls with Spicy Cucumber Sauce
Calamari Salad
Grilled Red Curry Beef and Potato Fajitas with
Lime Cucumber Raita
Jasmine Rice
Coconut Lime Pie

Table of Contents

Discover the Sights, Smells and Authentic Flavors of Thailand.

We hope you enjoy this first Thai Kitchen cookbook. It is based on our philosophy: to import only authentic, all natural Thai cooking products.

We use traditional family recipes to prepare our curry pastes and sauces. Grinding the spices, mixing and cooking are done in Bangkok, in small batches, the old-fashioned way. Thai Kitchen has made a serious commitment, in our entire line, to keep our products natural. No MSG, no artificial ingredients, preservatives or chemical additives. This commitment is shared by our suppliers and growers, who use healthy farming methods for the highest quality results.

Appetizers & Savory Snacks

Thais don't separate their meals into separate courses; they bring all the dishes to the table and enjoy them together, "family-style." The dishes we compartmentalize into appetizers, entrees and soups are brought to the table together and enjoyed as a complete meal.

Thais also like snacks and treats anytime of day. In their hot, tropical climate, eating light is sensible. Some of the recipes in this section are pleasant ideas for lunch. Treat yourself or your guests to many different Thai flavors by serving a few appetizers and snacks together for a wonderful meal.

Chicken, Pork, or Beef Satay

This is one dish everyone agrees to share at a Thai restaurant. The effort to make it from scratch is really minimal -- it can marinate in the refrigerator overnight so you can impress your guests in a snap.

    3 cloves garlic
    ½ cup Thai Kitchen Pure Coconut Milk (Regular or Lite)
    2 Tbs. Thai Kitchen Red Curry Paste
    2 Tbs. Thai Kitchen Premium Fish Sauce
    8 oz. thinly sliced chicken, pork, or beef
    bamboo skewers*
    Thai Kitchen Peanut Satay Sauce (Original Recipe or Spicy)

Make the marinade: In a blender or food processor, puree the garlic, coconut milk, red curry paste and fish sauce.

Skewer the meat and place in a shallow dish. Cover with the marinade and refrigerate 4 hours or overnight. Barbecue or broil the skewered meat for 2 to 3 minutes per side, until meat is browned and cooked. Serve with Thai Kitchen Peanut Satay Sauce on the side. Makes 8 to 10 skewers.

---

* Bamboo skewers are usually pre-soaked in water to prevent their burning off during cooking. This is not necessary here, since the skewers soak in the marinade with the meat.

Crispy Fish Cakes

Thais love fish, in any form, at any time of the day. These crisp and spicy patties could serve as an appetizer, a snack, a hot or cold lunch dish.

12 oz. firm white fish fillet
1 Tbs. Thai Kitchen Red Curry Paste
1 egg
8 green beans, thinly sliced or slivered
4 green onions, tops only, thinly sliced
3 kaffir lime leaves*, minced
3 cloves garlic, minced
2 Tbs. Thai Kitchen Premium Fish Sauce
1 tsp. sugar
1 ½ Tbs. cornstarch
2 Tbs. vegetable oil
Cucumber Relish (see page 113), Spicy Cucumber Sauce (see
        Fusion section, page 144), *or* Thai Kitchen Spicy Thai
        Chili Sauce

Cube fish. In a food processor combine fish, red curry paste and egg and blend until smooth. Set aside. In a bowl, combine green beans, green onions, kaffir lime leaves and garlic; with a spoon or fork mix lightly. Add fish sauce, sugar and cornstarch and blend together well to make a smooth paste. Combine this mixture with the processed fish mixture. Mix well to combine all ingredients.

Heat a wok or heavy skillet to medium-high heat and add oil. With lightly moistened hands, form ¼ cup portions of the fish mixture into patties (small, flat pancakes) and slide them into the oil. Don't crowd the pan; cook a few at a time. Fry until golden brown on one side, then turn and cook until other side is golden brown. Do not overcook. Drain on absorbent paper towels. Serve warm or cold with Cucumber Relish or Spicy Cucumber Sauce. For a quick topping, splash on Thai Kitchen Spicy Thai Chili Sauce. Makes 6 servings.

Note: To test mixture for flavor and texture, make a small ball and drop it into boiling water or fry in hot oil. If you want firmer patties, add more fish or egg. For a softer consistency add more cornstarch or a small amount of heavy cream.

* Kaffir lime leaves are optional in this recipe. See, Kaffir Lime Leaves, page 193.

Spicy Clams with Basil

In Thailand, this is served as an appetizer or snack, rather than an entree.

16 oz. fresh small clams
1 Tbs. vegetable oil
1 medium shallot, chopped
1 Tbs. fresh ginger, thinly sliced or slivered
2 cloves garlic, chopped
2 Tbs. chopped Thai basil
1 Tbs. Thai Kitchen Premium Fish Sauce
2 Tbs. Thai Kitchen Spicy Thai Chili Sauce
1 cup clam broth (or reserve cooking water)
2 tsp. cornstarch, dissolved in 1 Tbs. water
salt and freshly ground white pepper to taste
Optional garnish: sprigs of fresh basil

Plunge clams into a pot of rapidly boiling water. Remove as soon as they open up and plunge them into cold water. (Reserve 1 cup of the cooking water as your broth if you do not have clam broth.) Rinse well and set aside.

In a wok or heavy skillet, heat oil and sauté shallot, ginger and garlic for 1 to 2 minutes. Stir in basil, fish sauce and chili sauce; cook for two minutes. Add broth and bring to a boil. Blend in cornstarch mixture and stir until sauce thickens. Season to taste with salt and pepper. Add clams and toss lightly to coat. Place on a platter and garnish with sprigs of fresh basil. Makes 4 servings.

Crispy Fried Tofu

These tasty protein-rich strips are like vegetarian nuggets. Serve as an anytime snack with a savory sauce or dressing.

8 oz. firm tofu
¼ cup rice flour
2 Tbs. cornstarch
5 cups vegetable oil for deep frying
Thai Kitchen Red Chili Dipping Sauce
Thai Kitchen Peanut Satay Sauce (Original Recipe or Spicy)
lettuce leaves
cucumber, slices
Optional garnish: sprigs of fresh cilantro

Drain tofu. Remove from container and wrap tightly in a dry cloth to remove moisture; let stand for 20 minutes. Cut tofu into strips 2"x1"x¼". Combine rice flour and cornstarch. Coat tofu with flour mixture.

In a wok on medium heat, preheat oil for deep frying. Deep fry strips at 385°F for 7 to 8 minutes or until golden brown. Drain on absorbent paper. Serve with Thai Kitchen Red Chili Dipping Sauce and Peanut Satay Sauce, lettuce leaves and cucumber on the side. Garnish with sprigs of fresh cilantro. Makes 3 to 4 servings.

Thai Barbecued Chicken Pizza

California claims to have invented Barbecued Chicken Pizza. Our version uses rich, spicy Thai seasonings and sauces to give the dish a brilliant new flavor. Serve as an entree or an appetizer.

> 1 lb. boneless, skinless chicken breasts
> 6 to 8 bamboo skewers for pre-grilling chicken
> ½ cup Thai Kitchen Pure Coconut Milk (Regular or Lite)
> 1 Tbs. brown sugar
> 1 Tbs. Thai Kitchen Premium Fish Sauce
> 2 tsp. ground coriander
> 1 tsp. freshly ground black pepper
> 1 to 2 Tbs. Thai Kitchen Red Chili Paste
> 2 pizza crusts, 10" each (from scratch or packaged)
> ½ cup Thai Kitchen Peanut Satay Sauce (Original Recipe or
>   Spicy)
> 2 Tbs. additional coconut milk to drizzle over top of pizza
> *Optional garnish:* sprigs of fresh cilantro

Early in the day or day before: Cut chicken into 1" cubes. In a small bowl or sealable plastic bag, combine coconut milk, sugar, fish sauce, coriander, black pepper and red chili paste. Mix until well blended. Add chicken cubes to marinade and refrigerate at least 1 to 1 ½ hours. While chicken is marinating, pre-soak bamboo skewers in water, about an hour, to prevent them from burning off. Thread marinated chicken onto skewers, about 3 to 4 pieces per skewer. Broil until partially cooked and beginning to brown lightly on both sides, about 1 or 2 minutes per side. Baste with remaining marinade. Refrigerate until ready to assemble.

Prepare two 10" pizza crusts following your own recipe or the recipe from the package of pre-made dough (or use pre-made, pre-packaged pizza crusts from your supermarket).

Topping the pizza: Cut each barbecued chicken cube in half. Spread a thin layer of peanut satay sauce evenly on each crust. Evenly distribute chicken pieces over each crust. Bake each pizza separately, one at a time, in the middle rack of a 350°F oven for 7 to 8 minutes or until crust is nicely browned. Remove from oven and drizzle with additional coconut milk. Top with torn sprigs of fresh cilantro. Makes two 10-inch pizzas.

Bangkok Seafood Cocktail

Delicious, elegant and a snap to make.

8 oz. cooked shrimp, shelled and deveined
¼ cup fresh cilantro, coarsely chopped
2-3 Tbs. Thai Kitchen Red Chili Dipping Sauce
juice of ½ lime
2 cups iceberg or head lettuce, coarsely chopped
Optional garnish: 2 lime wedges

Combine the shrimp, cilantro, red chili dipping sauce and lime juice in a small bowl. Arrange the chopped lettuce on 2 small plates. Serve the seafood cocktail over the lettuce and garnish with lime wedges. Makes 2 servings.

Bangkok Wings

A low-fat twist on the Buffalo original.

 1 lb. chicken wings
 6 Tbs. Thai Kitchen Thai Barbecue Sauce
 1 Tbs. fresh lemon juice
 1 Tbs. apple cider vinegar
 2 Tbs. vegetable oil

In a bowl, combine the barbecue sauce, lemon juice, vinegar and oil. Place the wings on a hot grill and baste both sides with the sauce. Barbecue the wings for 7-10 minutes, turn and baste, and grill for an additional 7-10 minutes basting frequently. Serve hot or cold with extra Thai Kitchen Thai Barbecue Sauce on the side. Makes 3 to 4 servings.

Spicy Thai Pumpkin Nuts

An exotic treat to serve with cocktails.

2 cups fresh pumpkin seeds (available in bulk in many natural food stores or substitute almonds, pecans or walnuts)
1 tsp. peanut oil or vegetable oil
½ tsp. salt
2 Tbs. Thai Kitchen Spicy Thai Chili Sauce

Preheat oven to 350°F. Wash the pumpkin seeds and completely remove any pulp. Pat the seeds dry with a paper towel. In a small bowl, combine the oil, salt and chili sauce. Add the pumpkin seeds and toss well to coat. Spread the seeds out on a cookie sheet and bake for 10-15 minutes, until the seeds turn golden. Be careful not to burn them. Makes 4 to 6 servings.

Thai Ceviche

There's a hint of curry in our version of South America's marinated raw fish dish! The citric acid from the lime juice will "cook" the fish for you. Buy the fillets from a market that specializes in very fresh fish, and tell them it's for ceviche.

8 oz. swordfish, tombo ahi or other sashimi grade fish fillet
¼ cup fresh lime juice
2 tsp. salt
1 tsp. Thai Kitchen Green Curry Paste
¼ cup Thai Kitchen Pure Coconut Milk (Regular or Lite)
¼ cup Thai Kitchen Lemon Grass Splash
2 Tbs. thinly sliced green onion
2 Tbs. fresh cilantro, chopped
1 small tomato, cut into ½" cubes
1 small avocado, cut into ½" cubes

Cut fish into ½" cubes (use only very fresh fish). In a glass bowl combine with lime juice and salt; toss lightly to mix. Be sure fish is covered with the juice. Marinate fish for at least 4 hours, tossing occasionally. Fish will become opaque and lose its raw look. Drain fish and discard lime juice. In a bowl whisk together green curry paste and coconut milk until green curry paste is fully dissolved. Add fish, lemon grass splash, green onion, cilantro, tomato and avocado; toss lightly. Refrigerate for 1 hour for flavors to blend. Serve chilled. Makes 4 servings.

Soups

Smooth coconut milk, lemon grass and herb-infused broth are starting points for traditional Thai soups. Thais have a terrific version of chicken noodle soup and every family has its own secret recipe for the ever-popular Coconut Ginger Soup known as *Tom Kha Gai*. Soup is brought to the table along with the rest of the meal, not eaten as a separate course. You will find many of these soups filling enough to be enjoyed as a complete meal.

Thai Soup Stock

Your basic stock for many Thai recipes. Freezes well.

8 cups water
1 lb. chicken bones
1 onion, quartered
2 oz. fresh cilantro with roots, coarsely chopped
2 stalks fresh lemon grass*, bruised
2 kaffir lime leaves**
1 Tbs. chopped ginger
½ tsp. salt
½ tsp. whole black peppercorns

In a large stock pot, combine all the ingredients. Bring to a boil. Reduce heat and simmer for 1 hour. Skim the surface to remove any film from the soup. Makes 2 - 4 servings.

* See, Lemon Grass, pages 194, 199.
** Kaffir lime leaves are optional in this recipe. See, Kaffir Lime Leaves, page 193.

Thai Pumpkin Bisque

A sumptuous hot-or-cold soup that blends pureed pumpkin and coconut milk with a tingling touch of chili. One taste and you know you're not in New England anymore!

1 ¼ lbs. pumpkin (or other winter squash)
2 cloves garlic, crushed
2 shallots, sliced
2 pieces fresh lemon grass*, cut in half and bruised
2 cups chicken broth
2 Tbs. Thai Kitchen Roasted Chili Paste
2 kaffir lime leaves**, broken in half
1 (14 oz.) can Thai Kitchen Pure Coconut Milk (Regular or Lite)
2 Tbs. Thai Kitchen Premium Fish Sauce
1 tsp. sugar
white pepper to taste
Optional garnishes: sprigs of fresh cilantro and 2 small red
          chilies, seeded and thinly sliced

Peel pumpkin and cut into ½" cubes. In a food processor, or with mortar and pestle, grind garlic, shallots and lemon grass into a paste. In a wok or large skillet, bring chicken broth to a boil. Add garlic mixture, chili paste and kaffir lime leaves; stir to dissolve chili paste. Add pumpkin and simmer for 15 minutes or until pumpkin is tender. Stir in coconut milk and return to a simmer. Add fish sauce, sugar and white pepper. Simmer for an additional 5 minutes. Remove any large pieces of lemon grass and kaffir lime leaves. Cool slightly and puree in a food processor or blender. Serve warm or chilled. Garnish with red chilies and sprigs of fresh cilantro leaves. Makes 6 servings.

Note: Shredded cooked chicken or small cooked shrimp could be sprinkled on the surface of the bisque as a garnish. Laotians make this soup without the coconut milk and usually add chunks of fish (like catfish).

* Lemon grass is optional in this recipe. See, Lemon Grass, pages 194, 199.
** Kaffir lime leaves are optional in this recipe. See, Kaffir Lime Leaves, page 193.

Thai Gazpacho

A colorful and refreshing cold soup. Use vegetable broth instead of chicken broth to make it all-vegetarian.

1 Tbs. peanut or vegetable oil
¼ cup chopped shallots
1 tsp. chopped garlic
½ " piece fresh galangal (Thai ginger) or Chinese ginger, sliced and bruised
2 cups chicken broth
1 ½ lbs. fresh tomatoes (or good quality canned), seeded and coarsely chopped
3 Tbs. Thai Kitchen Lemon Grass Salad Splash
1 tsp. salt
¼ cup fresh cilantro, coarsely chopped
2 Tbs. green onions, coarsely chopped
2 Tbs. Thai Kitchen Thai Barbecue Sauce
2 tsp. mint, coarsely chopped
1 cup cucumber, seeded and chopped
Optional garnishes: sprigs of leftover fresh cilantro and cucumber slices

Heat oil in a wok or skillet and sauté shallots until translucent. Add garlic and galangal and sauté 1 minute or until aromatic. Add chicken broth and 1 lb. of the tomatoes, and bring to a boil. Simmer for 20 minutes, then cool to room temperature.

Strain mixture, separating the pulp and the liquid. Reserve the liquid and set aside. To the strained pulp, add the remaining ½ lb. chopped tomatoes, lemon grass salad splash, salt, cilantro, green onions, barbecue sauce, mint and cucumber. Transfer to a food processor or blender.

Lightly chop mixture, using a pulsing action, to desired consistency. Combine this mixture with reserved liquid and chill thoroughly. Pour into individual bowls and garnish with sprigs of fresh cilantro and cucumber slices. Makes 6 to 8 servings.

Breakfast Rice Soup

This is the Thai idea of a hot breakfast, and a good way to use up leftover rice. If you're not ready for a spicy porridge in the morning, serve it as a light lunch or an evening meal. Think of this dish as the Thai version of a warm bowl of oatmeal.

2 cups Thai Soup Stock (see page 15) or chicken broth
2 stalks celery, thinly sliced
2 tsp. fresh ginger, minced
¼ tsp. white pepper
4 oz. pork, minced, or coarsely chopped chicken meat
1 cup cooked Thai Kitchen Jasmine Rice
2 Tbs. Thai Kitchen Premium Fish Sauce
1 Tbs. vegetable oil
2 cloves garlic, thinly sliced
Optional garnish: sprigs of fresh cilantro

In a medium saucepan, heat stock to a boil and add celery, ginger and white pepper. Add the meat, a little at a time, so meat is broken up. Stir in cooked rice and fish sauce and simmer about 5 to 7 minutes or until meat is cooked.

In a small skillet, heat oil to medium-high heat and fry garlic until golden brown and crisp. Drain on absorbent paper towels. (This can be done in advance or the day before). Ladle hot soup into bowls and sprinkle with crisp garlic; garnish with cilantro. Makes 4 servings.

Sour Prawn Soup

Among the delicacies caught off Thailand's Gulf Coast are the giant shrimp that are dignified with the name of prawns. However, any large shrimp will do for this flavorful and filling soup. Make the soup a main course by serving it over a mound of cooked Thai Kitchen Jasmine Rice.

12 oz. prawns (large shrimp)
2 tsp. Thai Kitchen Green Curry Paste
4 oz. straw mushrooms
½ cup green (unripe) papaya or carrot, shredded
½ cup green beans, cut into 1" pieces
1 cup Chinese cabbage, cut into 1" pieces
2 Tbs. tamarind paste*
1 Tbs. brown sugar
1 Tbs. Thai Kitchen Premium Fish Sauce

In a wok or large saucepan, simmer prawns in enough water to cover, until cooked or orange-pink in color, about 1-2 minutes. Cool prawns in the stock, then peel. Reserve 2 cups of the stock. Set aside.

Heat the reserved 2 cups of stock in a wok or saucepan over high heat. Stir in green curry paste. Add mushrooms, green papaya, green beans and Chinese cabbage. Bring to a boil, reduce heat and simmer until vegetables are just tender. Stir in tamarind paste, sugar and fish sauce. Place your desired amount of prawns into each bowl and ladle in soup. Makes 4 servings.

* See, Tamarind, Juice/Paste, page 195.

Hot & Sour Soup *(Tom Yum Soup)*

This is one of Thailand's most famous soups. Some say it helps cure colds. The soothing soup is our version of grandmother's chicken soup.

12 oz. chicken, or cleaned shrimp, shelled and deveined, or firm
      tofu, strained and cubed
3 cups chicken or vegetable stock
3 pieces fresh lemon grass*, cut in half and bruised
2-3 Tbs. Thai Kitchen Premium Fish Sauce
1/3 cup fresh lime juice
2 kaffir lime leaves**
1" piece fresh galangal (Thai ginger) or Chinese ginger, sliced
      and bruised
2 Tbs. sugar
2 Tbs. Thai Kitchen Tom Yum Hot & Sour Soup Mix
2 Tbs. Thai Kitchen Roasted Red Chili Paste
1 (15 oz.) can straw mushrooms, drained
Optional garnish: sprigs of fresh cilantro

Bone and skin the chicken; cut into large pieces. In a large pot, combine the stock, lemon grass, fish sauce, lime juice, kaffir lime leaves, galangal and sugar. Bring to a boil over high heat, then reduce heat and simmer for 15 minutes. Add tom yum hot & sour soup mix and roasted red chili paste and stir well to incorporate. Add the mushrooms and the chicken and simmer for an additional 10-15 minutes until chicken is cooked. (If using shrimp or tofu, simmer for an additional 10 minutes then add into soup. Cook until shrimp turns orange-pink in color or tofu is tender, about 1-2 minutes.) Remove lemon grass, kaffir lime leaves and galangal from soup before serving. Garnish with cilantro. Serves 4.

* See, Lemon Grass, pages 194, 199.
** Kaffir lime leaves are optional in this recipe. See, Kaffir Lime Leaves, page 193.

--- Thai Kitchen Cookbook: Soups ---

Coconut Ginger Soup (Tom Kha Gai)

One of Thailand's signature soups. This savory dish incorporates all of the exciting flavors of Thai cuisine. Rich and satisfying, it's a delicious addition to any feast, Thai or western.

12 oz. chicken, or cleaned shrimp, shelled and deveined, or firm tofu, strained and cubed
1 (14 oz.) can Thai Kitchen Pure Coconut Milk (Regular or Lite)
½ cup water
3 pieces fresh lemon grass*, cut in half and bruised
6 Tbs. Thai Kitchen Premium Fish Sauce
1/3 cup fresh lime juice
2 kaffir lime leaves**
1" piece fresh galangal (Thai ginger) or Chinese ginger, sliced and bruised
2 Tbs. sugar
2 Tbs. Thai Kitchen Tom Yum Hot & Sour Soup Mix
2 Tbs. Thai Kitchen Roasted Red Chili Paste
1 (15 oz.) can straw mushrooms, drained
Optional garnish: sprigs of fresh cilantro

Bone and skin chicken; cut into large bite-size cubes. In a large pot, combine the coconut milk, water, lemon grass, fish sauce, lime juice, kaffir lime leaves, galangal and sugar. Bring to a boil over high heat, then reduce heat and simmer for 15 minutes. Add tom yum hot & sour soup mix and roasted red chili paste and stir well to incorporate. Add the mushrooms and chicken, shrimp or tofu; simmer for an additional 10 minutes. Remove lemon grass, kaffir lime leaves and galangal from soup before serving. Garnish with cilantro. Makes 3 to 4 servings.

* See, Lemon Grass, pages 194, 199.
** Kaffir lime leaves are optional in this recipe. See, Kaffir Lime Leaves, page 193.

Chicken Noodle Soup with Cabbage
(Sen Mee Gai)

A light but very filling soup. Thais serve this with a small dish of sliced chili peppers on the side.

4 cups chicken stock
2 Tbs. Thai Kitchen Premium Fish Sauce
1 Tbs. Thai Kitchen Tom Yum Hot & Sour Soup Mix
1 clove garlic, finely chopped
1 tsp. vegetable oil
½ lb. ground turkey, fat-free or low-fat
2 cups Napa cabbage or Chinese cabbage, coarsely chopped
4 oz. (approx. half package) Thai Kitchen Thin Rice Noodles*
Optional garnish: chopped Thai chili peppers (or any hot chili
     such as jalapeno) and/or chopped fresh cilantro

Combine the chicken stock, fish sauce, tom yum hot & sour soup mix and garlic in a large saucepan and bring to a simmer over medium heat. In a small frying pan or wok, heat the oil and add the ground turkey. Cook over medium high heat until thoroughly cooked and no pink is left in the meat, about 5-7 minutes. Add the turkey, chopped cabbage and noodles to the soup and simmer for 10 minutes. Serve immediately with optional garnishes on the side. Serves 2 to 3.

* NOTE: For less starchy noodles that do not clump and stick together, soak noodles in hot tap water for 5 minutes. Rinse with cold water. Drain all water before adding to soup for cooking. See, Rice Noodle Preparation, page 201.

Tom Yum Carrot Soup

The delicious and exotic combination of fragrant galangal and lemon grass will put this soup on your menu every week!

2 Tbs. vegetable oil
2-4 Tbs. Thai Kitchen Tom Yum Hot & Sour Soup Mix
2 cups yellow onion, coarsely chopped
2 tsp. salt
2 tsp. brown sugar
4 cups carrots, coarsely chopped
2 pieces fresh lemon grass*, cut in half and bruised
2 Tbs. minced fresh galangal (Thai ginger) or Chinese ginger
¼ cup fresh lime juice
4 cups vegetable stock
1 (14 oz.) can Thai Kitchen Pure Coconut Milk (Regular or Lite)
Optional garnish: ¼ cup fresh cilantro

In a large 4 quart pot, heat the oil over medium high heat. Add the tom yum hot & sour soup mix, onions, salt and sugar and sauté for 5 minutes, until the onions are soft and fragrant. Add the carrots, lemon grass, galangal, lime juice, vegetable stock and coconut milk and simmer for 20-30 minutes. Remove the lemon grass and, in batches, purée the soup in a blender or food processor until smooth. Garnish with cilantro and serve immediately. Serves 4.

* Lemon grass is optional in this recipe. See, Lemon Grass, pages 194, 199.

Thai Squash Soup

This fragrant soup requires a few steps to prepare but is very easy to make. Steam the squash while you put together a salad, and dinner is on the table in a flash.

1 butternut squash
1 (14 oz.) can Thai Kitchen Pure Coconut Milk (Regular or Lite)
1 cup chicken or vegetable stock
1 Tbs. Thai Kitchen Tom Yum Hot & Sour Soup Mix
1 Tbs. Thai Kitchen Roasted Red Chili Paste
2 tsp. brown sugar
½ tsp. salt
Optional: 2 pieces lemon grass*, bruised
Optional garnish: ¼ cup fresh cilantro, chopped

Quarter the squash and remove the seeds. Steam the squash over boiling water for 15 minutes, until the squash is soft. Scrape the squash away from the tough rind and set aside. In a 2 quart saucepan, simmer the coconut milk, stock, tom yum hot & sour soup mix, roasted red chili paste, brown sugar, salt and optional lemon grass for 5 minutes. While the coconut milk mixture is simmering, purée the squash in a food processor, blender, or with a potato masher. Add the squash purée to the coconut milk mixture and stir well to combine. Simmer for 5 minutes and garnish with optional cilantro. Remove the lemon grass sections and serve immediately. Serves 4.

* See, Lemon Grass, pages 194, 199.

Salads

Hot weather calls for refreshing salads, and Thai chefs have made an art of them. With so many luscious fruits and vegetables available, many composed salads are crisp, colorful masterpieces. Salads are part of almost every meal, served not as a separate course but along with the other dishes as entrees. Thais use beef and pork, seafood and poultry, and combine these with fiery chilies, cool mint and savory cilantro. Salads are also a smart way to use small amounts of leftover grilled meats or seafood. These are substantial enough to enjoy as a meal on their own and can be made ahead of time – perfect for today's busy schedules.

Lemon Grass Splash Beef Salad

The zingy taste in this robust salad comes from chilies in the marinade.
Salad dressing in the marinade adds to the refreshing flavor.

1 bottle (7 oz.) Thai Kitchen Lemon Grass Salad Splash
3 tablespoons Thai Kitchen Premium Fish Sauce
1 clove garlic, minced
1 small red chili pepper, seeded and minced
2 (8 oz. each) sirloin steaks
½ cucumber
½ red onion, finely sliced
1 small red bell pepper, seeded and julienned
Optional garnishes: sprigs of fresh cilantro, mint leaves, small
      red chili peppers, thinly sliced

In a small bowl combine lemon grass salad splash, fish sauce, garlic and minced chili pepper; blend well. Pour ½ of the mixture over the steaks and marinate, refrigerated, for at least 2 hours. Reserve the remaining marinade mixture to use as a dressing for the salad.

Pan fry or broil the steaks to medium-rare. Let sit for 10 to 15 minutes. Then thinly slice beef and place in a large bowl. Cut cucumber in half lengthwise, then thinly slice crosswise. Combine steak, cucumber, onion, bell pepper and remaining marinade mixture; toss lightly. Serve at room temperature and accompany with sprigs of fresh cilantro, mint leaves and chili peppers. Makes 4 to 6 servings.

Hot & Sour Pork Salad

Pork and eggplant combine in a warm salad that's slightly sweet and just spicy enough. Serve on lettuce leaves with refreshing slices of young papaya.

8 oz. boneless pork loin
Marinade (see recipe below)
1 lb. Japanese eggplants (4 small)
1 red bell pepper, seeded and cubed
2 shallots, thinly sliced
2 stalks lemon grass*, thinly sliced
3 kaffir lime leaves**, minced
2 small red or green chilies, seeded and finely chopped
2 Tbs. chicken broth
2 Tbs. lemon juice
1 Tbs. Thai Kitchen Red Chili Dipping Sauce
1 Tbs. Thai Kitchen Premium Fish Sauce
1 Tbs. sugar

Coarsely chop pork. Prepare the marinade and combine with pork. Marinate for 1 hour. Preheat broiler. Cut eggplant diagonally into ¼" thick slices. Arrange on a lightly oiled baking sheet and broil 4" to 6" from heat about 15 minutes or until golden brown, turning slices over once. Cool eggplant slightly and coarsely chop. In a skillet sauté pork, bell pepper, shallots and lemon grass with the juices of the marinade for about 3 to 4 minutes or until pork is cooked. Stir in eggplant, kaffir lime, chilies, broth, lemon juice, red chili dipping sauce, fish sauce, sugar; heat through and serve. Makes 4 to 6 servings.

Marinade:
2 cloves garlic, minced
1 Tbs. Chinese oyster flavored sauce
1 Tbs. Thai Kitchen Premium Fish Sauce
1 Tbs. soy sauce

Combine all ingredients and blend well.

* Lemon grass is optional in this recipe. See, Lemon Grass, pages 194, 199.
** Kaffir lime leaves are optional in this recipe. See, Kaffir Lime Leaves, page 193.

Chicken Salad *(Chiang Mai Style)*

Chiang Mai is a northern city known for serving up dishes in the style of its neighbor, Laos. The addition of red chili dipping sauce in this recipe changes the flavor of the dish and makes it a bit sweeter than the usual version. Very tasty.

4 chicken breasts (1 lb), boneless, skinless, cooked
4 shallots, thinly sliced
¼ cup green onions, thinly sliced
½ cup mint leaves, chopped
½ cup fresh cilantro, chopped
½ cup fresh lime juice
¼ cup Thai Kitchen Premium Fish Sauce
2–4 Tbs. Thai Kitchen Red Chili Dipping Sauce
lettuce leaves
Optional garnish: sprigs of leftover fresh mint

Coarsely chop cooked chicken. In a bowl, combine chicken, shallots, green onions, mint and cilantro; toss lightly. For the dressing, combine lime juice, fish sauce and red chili dipping sauce to taste; mix well. Pour half of the dressing over chicken mixture and toss lightly to mix. For each serving, place a scoop of salad in a lettuce leaf and top with mint leaves; roll up to eat. Serve at room temperature, accompanied by the remaining dressing. Makes 4 servings.

Shrimp & Papaya Salad with Thai Vinaigrette

A classic and elegant lunch salad.

8 oz. mixed greens (butter lettuce, arugula, frisee, watercress, etc.)
1 firm ripe papaya
½ cup pine nuts
16 oz. large shrimp (16 to 20), shelled and deveined with tail
     intact
salt and white pepper to taste
2 Tbs. vegetable oil
Thai Vinaigrette (see recipe below)
1 large red bell pepper, julienned
½ cup cilantro leaves, lightly packed

Rinse and dry mixed greens. Peel papaya and cut into quarters.
Remove seeds and cut each section into a fan or slices. Chill
greens and papaya. Roast pine nuts at 325°F until golden
brown. Watch them closely, since they tend to burn quickly.
Cool. Lightly season shrimp with salt and white pepper. Heat
oil in a wok or skillet and lightly sauté shrimp until flesh turns
orange-pink in color, about 1-2 minutes. Set aside to cool.
Prepare vinaigrette. When ready to serve place mixed greens on
four plates. Artfully arrange chilled papaya slices and shrimp on
top of the greens. Drizzle with Thai Vinaigrette. Sprinkle with
bell pepper and cilantro leaves. Accompany with remaining
vinaigrette. Makes 4 servings.

Thai Vinaigrette:
3 Tbs. fresh lime juice
2 Tbs. Thai Kitchen Premium Fish Sauce
2 Tbs. sugar
1 tsp. Thai Kitchen Spicy Thai Chili Sauce
2 green onions, minced
1 Tbs. fresh cilantro, minced
2 tsp. ginger, minced

Combine all ingredients in a jar and shake vigorously; set aside.

Mango Salad

Sweet and sour – the rich flavor of mango contrasted with hints of lemon and lime.

1 large mango, half ripe
1 Tbs. vegetable oil
2 cloves garlic, thinly sliced
4 oz. pork, coarsely chopped
2 Tbs. Thai Kitchen Lemon Grass Salad Splash
2 Tbs. fresh lime juice
2 Tbs. Thai Kitchen Premium Fish Sauce
1 tsp. sugar
2 Tbs. fresh mint leaves, torn
2 Tbs. roasted peanuts, crushed
Optional garnish: 1 to 2 small red chilies, thinly sliced

Peel and seed mango and cut into julienne strips. In a wok or skillet, heat oil to medium-high heat and fry garlic until golden brown and crisp. Drain on absorbent paper and set aside. Add pork and stir-fry until brown. Stir in lemon grass salad splash, lime juice, fish sauce and sugar and cook until sugar is dissolved. Just before serving combine pork mixture, mint leaves and mango; toss lightly. Place on serving platter and sprinkle with crisp garlic, crushed peanuts and chilies. Makes 4 servings.

Grapefruit & Shrimp Salad

This dish is traditionally made with pomello, which looks like an oversized green grapefruit. If you are lucky enough to find it in your grocery store or in an Asian market, use it in place of grapefruit. Pomello is sweeter than grapefruit with a delicious citrus scent.

2 grapefruit or pomello, peeled and cut into small chunks
12 oz. cooked large shrimp, shelled and deveined
1/3 cup mint, coarsely chopped
1/3 cup fresh cilantro, coarsely chopped
1 Tbs. Thai Kitchen Spicy Thai Chili Sauce (*or more to taste*)
2 Tbs. sugar
Optional garnish: 4 lettuce leaves

If using a pomello, peel and remove the bitter white pith, separate the segments, and use a knife and fingers to remove the membranes. Cut fruit into chunks. Combine all of the ingredients in a large mixing bowl. Place a lettuce leaf on each plate and serve the salad on top of the leaf. Serves 4.

Spicy Corn Salad

Brightly colored, vibrantly flavored, a make-ahead winner!

1 (12 oz.) bag frozen corn
½ cup red onion, finely chopped
1 cup red bell pepper, finely chopped
¼ cup fresh cilantro, finely chopped
1-2 Tbs. Thai Kitchen Spicy Thai Chili Sauce
3 Tbs. lime juice
1-2 Tbs. sugar

Bring a pot of water to boil, add the frozen corn and boil for 1-3 minutes, until warm. Drain the corn and place in a large mixing bowl. Add the red onion, bell pepper and cilantro and toss well. In a small dish, combine the spicy Thai chili sauce, lime juice and sugar and mix until sugar dissolves. Pour over the corn and toss well. Prepare at least 1 hour ahead to allow flavors to blend. Serves 4 to 6.

Spicy Thai Seafood Salad

A quick dish that is easy to prepare, beautiful to look at and even better when you combine two or more types of seafood.

> 3 Tbs. sugar
> 4 Tbs. Thai Kitchen Premium Fish Sauce
> 1/3 cup fresh lime juice
> 2 Tbs. Thai Kitchen Spicy Thai Chili Sauce (or more to taste)
> 12 oz. cooked large shrimp, shelled and deveined, scallops or
>   calamari rings (or a combination)
> ¼ cup fresh mint, coarsely chopped
> 1 small red onion, thinly sliced
> 2 green onions, chopped into ¼" rings
> 2 cucumbers, peeled and thinly sliced
> *Optional garnishes*: 4 large lettuce leaves and ¼ cup fresh
>   cilantro, coarsely chopped

In a small bowl, dissolve sugar in fish sauce, lime juice and spicy Thai chili sauce. In a large bowl, combine remaining ingredients and toss with liquid mixture. Serve on lettuce leaves and garnish with cilantro. Makes 2 to 4 servings.

Thai Potato Salad

Sure to become a family favorite on the Fourth of July menu!

2 lbs. new potatoes
2 tsp. salt
½ cup mayonnaise
1 Tbs. Thai Kitchen Red Curry Paste
1 Tbs. Thai Kitchen Lemon Grass Salad Splash
½ cup green onion, tops only, coarsely chopped
½ cup fresh cilantro, coarsely chopped

Bring a large pot of water to boil and add the potatoes and salt. Cook the potatoes 10-15 minutes, until a fork easily pierces the potato. Drain and set aside. In a large serving bowl, combine the mayonnaise, red curry paste, lemon grass salad splash, green onion and cilantro, mixing well. Once the potatoes have cooled to the touch, quarter them and add to the serving bowl. Toss well and serve at room temperature or cold. Makes 2 to 4 servings.

Bangkok Fruit Salad

Lime juice really brings out the exotic flavor of this salad. You may also use pineapple and banana in this fast and easy low-fat salad or dessert.

1 ripe papaya, seeded, peeled and cut into ½" cubes
1 ripe mango, peeled and cut into ½" cubes
3 Tbs. lime juice
¼ cup mint
Optional: 1 Tbs. Thai Kitchen Spicy Thai Chili Sauce for a
       unique Thai flavor
Optional garnish: sprigs of fresh cilantro

In a decorative serving bowl, combine the papaya, mango, lime juice, mint and optional spicy Thai chili sauce. Toss well to combine and garnish with cilantro sprigs. Serves 2 to 3.

Thai Cobb Salad

A new and delightful twist on the famous salad. Perfect with leftover grilled or barbecued chicken.

2 chicken breasts, boned and skinned
1 (7 oz.) package Thai Kitchen Thin Rice Noodles*
½ bunch basil
½ bunch fresh cilantro
10 cherry tomatoes, quartered
1 jar (8 oz.) Thai Kitchen Peanut Satay Sauce (Original Recipe or
        Spicy)
1 head Bibb or butter lettuce
Optional garnish: ¼ cup chopped peanuts

Heat oven to 350°F. Bake the chicken breasts for 20 to 30 minutes, until they are cooked through. Set aside to cool. Bring a large pot of water to a rolling boil. Break the noodles into small pieces, add them to the pot and boil for 2 minutes or until noodles are soft, but firm and not mushy. Stir noodles frequently while cooking to prevent clumping. Drain well with cold water. Cut the chicken into ½" pieces and put in a large mixing bowl. Coarsely chop the basil and cilantro and add to the mixing bowl. Add the noodles and quartered tomatoes and the peanut satay sauce. Toss the mixture until the dressing is evenly distributed. Divide the lettuce between 4 plates, and spoon equal portions of salad over the lettuce. Garnish with chopped peanuts and leftover cilantro.

* See, Rice Noodle Preparation, page 201.

Spicy Thai Salad Dressing

A spicy yet subtle dressing that blends hot, sweet & sour tastes. Gives an amazing new flavor to your favorite fresh greens.

> ½ - 1 Tbs. red chili pepper, finely minced
> 2 Tbs. rice vinegar
> 2 Tbs. fresh lime juice
> 1 Tbs. sugar
> 2 Tbs. Thai Kitchen Premium Fish Sauce
> ½ tsp. salt

In a pot, combine chili, vinegar, lime juice, sugar, fish sauce and salt. Bring to a simmer over low heat. Stir until sugar is dissolved. Cool and toss with your favorite salad greens or cold vegetables.

Beef, Pork & Fowl

Whether a rich Bangkok-style curry or a simple dish of grilled meat with dipping sauce, Thai Kitchen has collected a huge variety of chicken, beef, pork and seafood specialties from all around Thailand. The main dishes of Thai cuisine represent the wide variety of fresh ingredients available there. Meats are combined with vegetables and fruits, herbs and spices. Most are stir-fried or otherwise lightly cooked, using a minimum of oil. The result: a low-fat, nutrition rich cuisine, high on freshness and flavor.

Roasted Chili Flank Steak

The cold leftover steak will make fabulous next-day open face sandwiches.

2 Tbs. Thai Kitchen Roasted Red Curry Paste
2 Tbs. black peppercorns, crushed
1 Tbs. cumin seeds, crushed
½ Tbs. coarse sea salt
24 oz. flank steak
Fiery Thai Salsa (see page 111)
Thai Kitchen Jasmine Rice

In a small bowl, combine roasted red curry paste, black pepper, cumin and salt; blend well. Rub surface of steak with mixture to coat evenly and let sit for 30 minutes to 1 hour. Barbecue or broil 4 to 6 minutes each side for medium-rare or 6 to 8 minutes each side for medium. Let stand 5 minutes. Slice steak thinly across the grain. Serve accompanied with Fiery Thai Salsa and rice. Makes 4 servings.

Green Curry Beef

Slice the beef in the morning, refrigerate, then figure on just 20 minutes or less to stir up a robust beef dish for dinner.

8 oz. flank steak
½ tsp. salt
¼ tsp. white pepper
2 Tbs. vegetable oil
1 ½ Tbs. Thai Kitchen Green Curry Paste
1 stalk fresh lemon grass*, thinly sliced
2 kaffir lime leaves**
1 (14 oz.) can Thai Kitchen Pure Coconut Milk (Regular or Lite)
1 Tbs. Thai Kitchen Premium Fish Sauce
2 tsp. brown sugar
¼ cup thinly sliced basil
Thai Kitchen Jasmine Rice
Optional garnish: sprigs of fresh basil

Cut beef across the grain into thin slices and season with salt and white pepper. Heat oil in a wok or large skillet to medium-high heat. Add green curry paste and stir-fry for 30 to 60 seconds, until fragrant. Add beef, lemon grass and kaffir lime leaves and stir-fry for 2 to 3 minutes or until meat starts to brown. Add coconut milk and bring to a simmer, stirring frequently. Stir in fish sauce and brown sugar and simmer gently for 10 to 15 minutes. Sprinkle with sliced basil. Remove from heat, cover, and let stand for 3 minutes. Remove lemon grass and kaffir lime leaves. Serve over cooked Thai Kitchen Jasmine Rice. Garnish with sprigs of fresh basil. Makes 4 to 6 servings.

Note: If beef is partially frozen, it is easier to slice thinly.

* Lemon grass is optional in this recipe. See, Lemon Grass, pages 194, 199.
** Kaffir lime leaves are optional in this recipe. See, Kaffir Lime Leaves, page 193.

Gingered Pork with Barbecue Sauce

The combination of pork and fresh ginger is very popular in Northern Thailand. Barbecues are a specialty there and this version is not only rich and spicy – it's easy.

1 lb. boneless pork loin
1 Tbs. vegetable oil
2 Tbs. fresh ginger, minced
½ red bell pepper, cut into thin strips
¼ cup Thai Kitchen Thai Barbecue Sauce
2 Tbs. Thai Kitchen Premium Fish Sauce
½ tsp. ground white pepper
Optional garnish: sprigs of fresh cilantro

Cut pork into 1" cubes. Heat oil in a wok or large skillet to high heat. Add pork and ginger and stir-fry for 4 to 5 minutes or until pork is lightly browned. Add bell pepper, Thai barbecue sauce, fish sauce and white pepper and cook for 2 to 3 minutes. Place on a serving platter and garnish with sprigs of fresh cilantro. Makes 4 to 6 servings.

Sweet Pork

Hot or cold, sweet pork is the Asian version of versatile sugar-glazed ham.

1 lb. pork loin
½ cup sugar
¾ cup water, (divided)
2 Tbs. Thai Kitchen Premium Fish Sauce
1 Tbs. soy sauce (dark soy sauce preferred)
4 shallots, thinly sliced
1 Tbs. vegetable oil

Cut pork into ½" cubes. Set aside. In a skillet over medium-high heat, combine sugar and ¼ cup of the water and caramelize, stirring frequently, about 6 to 8 minutes or until light golden brown. Be careful that it does not burn. Stir in the pork and coat with this syrup. Stir in the remaining ½ cup water, fish sauce and soy sauce. Reduce heat and simmer for about 20 to 25 minutes or until pork is cooked and liquid is reduced to a light syrup. Remove from pan and set aside. Heat oil in skillet and fry shallots until golden brown and crisp. Serve sweet pork as a snack or an entree. Top with crisp shallots. Makes 4 to 6 servings.

Crispy Fried Beef

A crisp accompaniment or topping to any Thai dish.

24 oz. flank steak
3 Tbs. coriander seeds
1 tsp. white peppercorns
2 Tbs. garlic, minced
¼ cup Thai Kitchen Premium Fish Sauce
2 cups vegetable oil (for deep frying)
Thai Kitchen Jasmine Rice
Optional: Thai Kitchen Light Plum Spring Roll Sauce

Slice steak thinly into pieces about 1"x4"x1/8". With a mortar and pestle or spice grinder coarsely grind coriander seeds and white peppercorns. In a large bowl or sealable plastic bag combine beef, spice mixture, garlic and fish sauce. Marinate for 2 to 3 hours in the refrigerator, mixing occasionally. Turn oven to lowest setting (about 170°F). Place beef in a single layer on baking sheets covered with foil. Dry beef in the oven for 4 to 5 hours. Once dried, heat oil to high for deep frying and fry beef until brown. Drain on absorbent towels. Serve as a side dish with a curry and rice, or as a snack with Thai Kitchen Light Plum Spring Roll Sauce as a dip. Makes 6 to 8 servings.

Note: If beef is partially frozen, it is easier to slice thinly. Crisp fried beef will keep well in the refrigerator for 2 weeks.

Thai Barbecue Spareribs

Authentic Thai herbs and spices in our barbecue sauce give garlicky ribs a deep rich color and flavor, a spicy fragrance. Even Texans will want your recipe.

> 1" piece ginger, peeled and minced
> 4 cloves garlic, minced
> 2 kaffir lime leaves*, minced
> 1 tsp. Thai Kitchen Lemon Grass (Dried) or 2 stalks fresh lemon
>   grass**, minced
> 2 ½ to 3 lbs. pork spareribs
> 1 jar (7 oz.) Thai Kitchen Thai Barbecue Sauce

In a bowl, combine ginger, garlic, kaffir lime leaves and lemon grass; blend well. Rub mixture on both sides of the ribs. Cover and refrigerate for 1 to 2 hours or overnight. Preheat oven to 375°F. Brush both sides of spareribs with barbecue sauce. Roast for 40 minutes, turning once. Brush with additional barbecue sauce. This can be done in advance.

When ready to serve, barbecue or broil ribs for 15 to 20 minutes, basting occasionally and turning several times. Accompany with extra Thai Kitchen Thai Barbecue Sauce. Makes 4 to 6 servings.

* Kaffir lime leaves are optional in this recipe. See, Kaffir Lime Leaves, page 193.
** Lemon grass is optional in this recipe. See, Lemon Grass, pages 194, 199.

Masuman Beef Stew

The vegetables and potatoes reveal this mild stew's Indian origins. For truly authentic Southern Thai flavor, add the optional cinnamon and cardamom.

2 Tbs. vegetable oil
2 cups yellow onion, roughly chopped
2 tsp. salt (divided)
1 tsp. brown sugar
2 cloves garlic, finely chopped
2 Tbs. Thai Kitchen Roasted Red Chili Paste
1 cup flour
1 tsp. ground black pepper
1 tsp. Thai Kitchen Lemon Grass (Dried) or 1 stalk fresh lemon
    grass*, minced
1 lb. beef, cut into 1" cubes (try boneless chuck roast or rump
    roast)
1 large can (28 oz.) whole tomatoes
2 cups carrots, cut into ¼" pieces
2 cups potatoes, peeled and cut into ¼" chunks
1 to 1 ½ cups beef stock
Thai Kitchen Jasmine Rice or Stir-Fry Rice Noodles
Optional: ½ tsp. ground cinnamon and ½ tsp. ground
    cardamom

Heat the oil in a large, heavy bottomed stock pot over medium heat. Add the onion, 1 tsp. salt, and brown sugar and sauté until soft, about 5 minutes. Add the garlic and roasted red chili paste and sauté for an additional 2-3 minutes. In a small bowl, mix the flour, additional 1 tsp. salt, pepper and lemon grass. Coat the cubed meat, gently shaking off the excess flour, and add to the stock pot. Sauté for 5-7 minutes, until the meat begins to brown. Add the tomatoes, carrots, potatoes, 1 cup of stock and optional spices, reduce the heat to simmer and cook for 25-35 minutes. Check the stew and add additional stock if it starts to look dry. Serve over cooked Thai Kitchen Jasmine Rice, or Thai Kitchen Stir-Fry Rice Noodles tossed with butter and sesame seeds. Serves 4 to 6.

* Lemon grass is optional in this recipe. See, Lemon Grass, pages 194, 199.

Thai Peanut Stir-Fry

Satay sauce adds a luxurious touch to a fast and easy meal.

2 cloves garlic, finely minced
4 Tbs. vegetable oil (for stir-frying)
8 oz. beef, sliced
¼ cup sliced bamboo shoots*, rinsed and drained
1 green zucchini, sliced
1 red bell pepper, sliced
2 Tbs. Thai Kitchen Premium Fish Sauce
4 Tbs. Thai Kitchen Peanut Satay Sauce (Original Recipe or
    Spicy)

In a large wok or skillet, sauté garlic in vegetable oil over medium heat until the garlic is golden brown. Add the beef and stir-fry for 5-10 minutes. Add the bamboo shoots, zucchini, bell pepper, fish sauce and peanut satay sauce and stir-fry for another 5-10 minutes. Serves 2.

* Soak bamboo in water and salt for 20 minutes to minimize the can taste. Drain well with water before cooking.

Pork Loin with Chili Sauce *(Kaw Moo Yang)*

Marinating well in advance will make the pork loin moist and deeply flavorful.

4 cloves garlic
2 teaspoons black peppercorns
2 Tbs. fresh cilantro, chopped
2 Tbs. Chinese oyster flavored sauce
2 Tbs. soy sauce
1 ½ lbs. pork loin, sliced into ½" rounds (or boneless pork
        chops)
Sweet Chili Sauce (see page 115)

In a blender or with a mortar and pestle, combine the garlic, peppercorns, and cilantro. Pulse or grind into a thick paste. Turn into a large metal bowl and add the oyster flavored sauce and soy sauce and mix well to combine. Add the pork and marinate for 2-3 hours or overnight.

Grill the pork over hot coals or broil for 2-3 minutes on each side. Serve with the Sweet Chili Sauce. Serves 4 to 6.

Pork Stir-Fry with Fresh Mushrooms (*Moo Pad King*)

This dish is especially good made with a combination of fresh mushrooms, which come into season in the fall. Try brown mushrooms, oyster mushrooms, shiitakes, or thinly sliced portabello mushrooms.

2 Tbs. vegetable oil
2 Tbs. garlic, finely chopped
½ cup red onion, roughly chopped
½ tsp. salt
1 Tbs. brown sugar
2 Tbs. Thai Kitchen Roasted Red Chili Paste
1 Tbs. Thai Kitchen Premium Fish Sauce
2-3 Tbs. fresh lime juice
12 oz. pork, sliced into thin ½" strips
2 cups fresh mushrooms, cut into ¼" slices
1 cup red bell pepper, cut into ¼" slices
Optional: ¼ cup basil, coarsely chopped, and 2 Tbs. Thai
        Kitchen Spicy Thai Chili Sauce (for an extra kick)

Heat the oil in a wok or large skillet over medium high heat. Add the garlic, onion, salt and sugar and stir-fry for 2-3 minutes, until the onion is soft and the garlic begins to turn golden. Add the roasted red chili paste, fish sauce and lime juice and stir to combine. Add the pork and stir-fry for 3-5 minutes, until the pork is no longer pink. Add the mushrooms and red pepper and stir-fry for an additional 3-5 minutes, until the pepper has softened. Toss with optional basil and Spicy Thai Chili Sauce and serve immediately. Serves 4.

Pork Stir-Fry with Asparagus and Mint (Moo Pad Pow)

A delicious and colorful recipe that's ready in just minutes. Pork chops offer the best value: cut the meat away from the bone and slice into thin strips for this recipe.

 1 Tbs. vegetable oil
 2 Tbs. Thai Kitchen Roasted Red Chili Paste
 2 Tbs. Thai Kitchen Premium Fish Sauce
 2 tsp. sugar
 1 cup yellow onion, cut into thin, ¼" rings
 2 cups asparagus, zucchini or broccoli, cut into 1" pieces
 1 lb. pork, cut into thin strips (try pork loin or pork chops with
         the meat cut off the bone)
 ½ cup red bell pepper, cut into thin ¼" strips
 1/3 cup mint leaves, coarsely chopped

Heat the oil in a wok or frying pan over medium high heat. Add roasted red chili paste, fish sauce and sugar and stir well to combine, cooking for 1 minute. Add the onion and asparagus, stir-frying for 3 minutes. Cover the pan and let cook for an additional 3-5 minutes until the vegetables are tender. Remove the cover and add the pork and red bell pepper. Stir-fry for 2-3 minutes, until the pork is cooked completely. Add the mint, tossing well to combine, and serve. Serves 3 to 4.

Red Curry Pork with Tomatoes

Simmer and serve in just minutes.

1 (14 oz.) can Thai Kitchen Pure Coconut Milk (Regular or Lite)
½ cup chicken or vegetable stock
2 tsp. brown sugar
1 Tbs. Thai Kitchen Red Curry Paste
1 Tbs. Thai Kitchen Premium Fish Sauce
1 pint basket cherry tomatoes, stems removed, and halved
12 oz. pork (or you may substitute beef), cut into ½" slices
½ cup chopped snow peas
Thai Kitchen Jasmine Rice

In a 2 quart saucepan, simmer the coconut milk, stock, sugar, red curry paste, fish sauce and tomatoes over medium heat for 7-10 minutes. While the coconut milk mixture is simmering, slice the meat into ½" strips. Add to the curry and simmer for an additional 5-7 minutes, or until the meat is completely cooked. Add the snow peas, simmer for an additional minute and serve over cooked Thai Kitchen Jasmine Rice. Serves 3 to 4.

Herb-Grilled Chicken with Thai BBQ Sauce

Marinating overnight brings out the full flavor of the herbs and keeps the chicken juicy.

6 whole chicken legs (thigh and drumstick) (about 4 lbs.)
1/3 cup fresh cilantro leaves
1/3 cup basil leaves
2 Tbs. shallots, chopped
1 Tbs. fresh ginger, chopped
2 tsp. garlic, chopped
¼ cup Thai Kitchen Lemon Grass Salad Splash
½ cup Thai Kitchen Thai Barbecue Sauce
½ cup Thai Kitchen Pure Coconut Milk (Regular or Lite)
1 Tbs. Thai Kitchen Premium Fish Sauce

Score chicken by making shallow surface cuts in a diamond pattern. In a food processor combine cilantro, basil, shallots, ginger, garlic and lemon grass salad splash. Pulse several times, scraping sides down occasionally, until mixture is evenly minced. Reserve 2 tablespoons of the herb mixture. Combine the remaining herb mixture with Thai barbecue sauce, coconut milk and fish sauce; mix well. Pour sauce over chicken and mix well to coat. Marinate overnight in the refrigerator. Barbecue or broil at medium heat for 35 to 40 minutes, turning occasionally. Chicken is cooked when slightly charred and crisp on the outside and juices run clear when pierced with a knife. Immediately brush both sides of chicken with reserved herb mixture. Makes 4 to 6 servings.

BBQ Garlic Chicken

Sweet, sour, and spicy – perfectly balanced flavors give zesty new life to everyday barbecued chicken.

    5 lbs. chicken thighs
    ½ cup Thai Kitchen Lemon Grass Salad Splash (divided)
    ½ cup Thai Kitchen Light Plum Spring Roll Sauce (divided)
    1 Tbs. coriander seeds
    1 Tbs. minced garlic
    2 tsp. coarsely cracked black pepper
    1 ½ tsp. salt
    12 oz. Chinese cabbage (6 cups), thinly sliced

Place chicken in a bowl or sealable plastic bag. Combine ¼ cup of the lemon grass salad splash, ¼ cup of the light plum spring roll sauce, coriander, garlic, black pepper and salt; blend well. Pour over chicken and marinate overnight or at least 2 hours in the refrigerator, turning periodically. Barbecue or broil until chicken is tender and juices run clear, about 45 to 50 minutes, turning occasionally. Combine Chinese cabbage with the remaining ¼ cup lemon grass salad splash and ¼ cup spring roll sauce; toss lightly. Place Chinese cabbage on a serving platter and top with barbecued chicken. Makes 8 to 10 servings.

Roast Duck Curry

Duck is a favorite Thai fowl but roast chicken, though not as rich a meat, also makes a splendid curry.

1 roasted duck (about 3 lbs.)
1 Tbs. peanut or vegetable oil
1 tsp. fresh ginger, minced
4 kaffir lime leaves*, minced
3 Tbs. Thai Kitchen Red Curry Paste
3 Tbs. tomato paste
½ cup chicken broth
½ cup Thai Kitchen Pure Coconut Milk (Regular or Lite)
2 Tbs. Thai Kitchen Peanut Satay Sauce (Original Recipe or
    Spicy)
2 cups green beans, cut diagonally into 1" lengths
3 large tomatoes, cut into wedges
1 Tbs. chopped basil leaves
Thai Kitchen Jasmine Rice
Optional garnish: 10 whole basil leaves

To roast the duck: Set the oven at 350°F. Place duck in an uncovered roasting pan and roast about 1 hour, or until almost done. Remove duck from oven and cool. Strip off skin. Roasting the duck the day before can save you time. Also, a store bought lightly seasoned roast duck or chicken can be used.

Remove meat from duck and cut into bite-sized pieces. Set aside. In a wok or heavy skillet heat oil and briefly stir-fry ginger and kaffir lime leaves for 1 minute. Add red curry paste and tomato paste and stir-fry about 3 to 4 minutes or until deep red in color. Deglaze wok with chicken broth and add coconut milk, peanut satay sauce, green beans and tomatoes. Bring to a boil, then reduce heat and simmer about 3 minutes. Add duck meat and continue to cook another 3 to 5 minutes or until duck is heated through. Be careful not to overcook. Stir in chopped basil and serve with cooked Thai Kitchen Jasmine Rice. Garnish with whole basil leaves. Makes 4 to 6 servings.

* Kaffir lime leaves are optional in this recipe. See, Kaffir Lime Leaves, page 193.

Chicken & Broccoli in Peanut Sauce

You can prepare the simple sauce a day in advance. Just reheat before serving.

> 2 lbs. chicken breasts, boneless and skinless
> 1 Tbs. Thai Kitchen Red Curry Paste
> 2 tsp. fresh ginger, finely grated
> 1 tsp. garlic, crushed
> ½ cup Thai Kitchen Peanut Satay Sauce (Original Recipe or
>   Spicy)
> 2 Tbs. Thai Kitchen Premium Fish Sauce
> 1 (14 oz.) can Thai Kitchen Pure Coconut Milk (Regular or Lite)
> 4 cups broccoli florets
> *Optional garnish:* 2 Tbs. basil, chopped and 1 Tbs. green onion,
>   tops only, chopped

In a sealable plastic bag combine chicken, red curry paste, ginger and garlic. Massage bag until ingredients are well mixed and chicken is thoroughly coated. Refrigerate for 30 minutes. In a saucepan combine peanut satay sauce, fish sauce and coconut milk; blend well and cook until heated through. Broil chicken about 8 to 10 minutes, turning occasionally, until chicken is cooked. Meanwhile, blanch broccoli in boiling water; drain and set aside, keep warm. Arrange broccoli on a serving platter and top with chicken. Pour sauce over chicken and sprinkle with basil and green onion. Makes 6 servings.

Sweet & Sour Stir-Fry

A super fast stir-fry everyone loves.

2 Tbs. soy sauce
2-4 cloves garlic, finely minced
1 1" piece fresh ginger, finely minced
1-2 Tbs. Thai Kitchen Spicy Thai Chili Sauce
1 Tbs. vegetable oil
1 medium onion, cut into ½" chunks
1 lb. chicken breasts, boneless, skinless, cut into ½" chunks
1 green bell pepper, cut into ½" chunks
1 red bell pepper, cut into ½" chunks
1 (8 oz.) small can pineapple pieces
4-6 Tbs. Thai Kitchen Light Plum Spring Roll Sauce

Place the chicken in a small bowl with the soy sauce, garlic, ginger and spicy Thai chili sauce to marinate. Cut up the vegetables. Heat the oil in a large wok or skillet over medium high heat. Add the onion and stir-fry for 3 minutes. Add the chicken and stir-fry for 3-5 minutes. Add the green and red peppers, the pineapple and the light plum spring roll sauce and stir-fry for an additional 5 minutes or until the chicken is completely cooked. Serves 3 to 4.

Lemon Grass Chicken

This chicken is juicy and tender -- the leftovers are perfect for adding to our Thai Rice Salad.

> 2 tsp. Thai Kitchen Lemon Grass (Dried) or 1/3 cup fresh lemon
>   grass*, coarsely chopped
> 1 tsp. salt
> 2 cups yellow onion, coarsely chopped
> 1 chicken (3-4 lbs.), cut into pieces
> 1 lime, quartered
> 1 lemon, quartered
> Thai Kitchen Red Chili Dipping Sauce

Preheat the oven to 375°F. Combine the lemon grass, salt, onion and chicken and toss well. Squeeze the lemon and lime quarters over the chicken and toss again to evenly coat the chicken. Place in a roasting pan and cook for 35-45 minutes, until the chicken is completely cooked. Turn the chicken once or twice while cooking and baste with any pan juices. Place the chicken on a serving platter. Reserve the pan juices (skim off any oil) for a dipping sauce or gravy. Serve with Red Chili Dipping Sauce on the side. Serves 4 to 6.

---

* Although the recipe is called Lemon Grass Chicken, lemon grass is optional in this recipe. You will be able to prepare a tasty Thai chicken dish without it. See, Lemon Grass, pages 194, 199.

Green Curry with Basil (Keow Wan Gai)

Smooth and rich with a delicate hint of basil.

1 (14 oz.) can Thai Kitchen Pure Coconut Milk (Regular or Lite)
1-4 Tbs. Thai Kitchen Green Curry Paste
1/3 cup vegetable or chicken stock
2-3 Tbs. Thai Kitchen Premium Fish Sauce
2 Tbs. brown sugar
¼ cup chopped basil leaves
1 ½ cups assorted vegetables, cut into 1" pieces (try red bell
          pepper, zucchini, peas, or your favorite combination)
12 oz. chicken breast, cut into 1" pieces
Thai Kitchen Jasmine Rice

Mix the coconut milk, green curry paste, stock, fish sauce, brown sugar and basil in a 2 quart saucepan and bring to a boil. Reduce heat to low and simmer for 15 minutes. Add the vegetables and chicken and simmer for an additional 10 minutes, until the chicken is thoroughly cooked. Serve over cooked Thai Kitchen Jasmine Rice. Serves 4.

Seafood & Fish

Thailand is famous for its seafood. No wonder. It has two long coastlines along the southern peninsula: on the Gulf of Thailand and on the Indian Ocean. Village fishing boats bring in fish, rock lobsters, crabs, squid, shrimp, giant prawns, and scallops. These fresh gifts from the sea are often simply steamed or grilled. Coconut, which grows abundantly in the South, appears in many seafood dishes, its milk used to thicken soup and curries. Note: Thai seafood recipes may call for prawns. That name is sometimes given to larger shrimp. In Bangkok, they serve the most gigantic prawns available, often in a simple sauce or grilled over charcoal.

Spicy Shrimp in Coconut Milk

A smooth, rich party dish. Prepare shrimp and sauce early in the day and finish just before serving.

1 lb. large shrimp, shelled and deveined
2 Tbs. Thai Kitchen Spicy Thai Chili Sauce
1 cup Thai Soup Stock (see page 15) or chicken broth
2 medium tomatoes, chopped
2 kaffir lime leaves*
1 tsp. fresh lemon juice
1 tsp. brown sugar
2/3 cup Thai Kitchen Pure Coconut Milk (Regular or Lite)
Thai Kitchen Jasmine Rice
Optional garnish: finely chopped green onions

Combine shrimp and spicy Thai chili sauce; blend well to coat and set aside or refrigerate. In a wok or large skillet bring stock to a boil. Add tomatoes, kaffir lime leaves, lemon juice and sugar. Reduce heat and simmer for 8 to 10 minutes, until most of the liquid has evaporated. Stir in coconut milk and simmer for 4 minutes. Add shrimp and cook until orange-pink in color, about 1-2 minutes. Taste to see if more lemon juice, sugar or fish sauce is needed to balance flavors. Transfer to a warm serving dish, remove kaffir lime leaves. Garnish with green onions sprinkled over the top of dish. Serve with cooked Thai Kitchen Jasmine Rice. Serves 4 to 6.

* Kaffir lime leaves are optional in this recipe. See, Kaffir Lime Leaves, page 193.

Red Curry Shrimp

Thai Kitchen makes red curry paste the traditional way: in small batches that taste as fresh as homemade. We take the labor out of cooking authentic curry.

> 1 (14 oz.) can Thai Kitchen Pure Coconut Milk (Regular or Lite), (divided)
> 1 ½ Tbs. Thai Kitchen Red Curry Paste
> 1 Tbs. brown sugar
> 2 kaffir lime leaves*, minced
> 1 lb. large shrimp, shelled and deveined
> 2 Tbs. Thai Kitchen Premium Fish Sauce
> ¼ cup basil, chopped
> Thai Kitchen Jasmine Rice
> *Optional garnishes*: sprigs of fresh basil and red chilies, thinly sliced

In a wok or heavy skillet heat half a can of the coconut milk. Stir in red curry paste and cook until well blended. Add the remaining coconut milk, brown sugar and kaffir lime leaves and bring to a boil. Reduce heat and simmer for 5 minutes. Add shrimp, and cook until shrimp are orange-pink in color, about 1-2 minutes. Stir in fish sauce and chopped basil. Place on a serving platter and garnish with sprigs of fresh basil and red chilies. Serve with cooked Thai Kitchen Jasmine Rice. Makes 4 to 6 servings.

* Kaffir lime leaves are optional in this recipe. See, Kaffir Lime Leaves, page 193.

Fish in Coconut-Tamarind Sauce

The sour-fruity taste of tamarind combined with mildly sweet coconut milk and hot red curry paste – plain fish never tasted so glamorous!

24 oz. swordfish, red snapper or other firm white fish fillet
1 cup Thai Kitchen Pure Coconut Milk (Regular or Lite)
2 tsp. Thai Kitchen Red Curry Paste
¼ cup tamarind paste*
¼ cup Thai Kitchen Premium Fish Sauce
2 Tbs. palm sugar or brown sugar
2 kaffir lime leaves**, minced
Thai Kitchen Jasmine Rice, cooked
Optional garnish: sprigs of fresh cilantro

Cut fish into 1" cubes; set aside. In a medium saucepan, combine coconut milk and red curry paste and simmer for 5 minutes, stirring occasionally, until red curry paste is dissolved. Stir in tamarind paste, fish sauce, sugar and kaffir lime leaves and simmer for 5 minutes. Add fish and simmer for 7 to 8 minutes or until fish is cooked and becomes opaque. Serve with cooked Thai Kitchen Jasmine Rice. Garnish with sprigs of fresh cilantro. Makes 4 to 6 servings.

* See, Tamarind, Juice/Paste, page 195.
** Kaffir lime leaves are optional in this recipe. See, Kaffir Lime Leaves, page 193.

Steamed Salmon with Thai Herbs

If you don't have a bamboo steamer, this dish is reason enough to buy one. Steaming is an age old method of cooking and the fish takes on the vibrant flavors of the herbs it is steamed with. The fish is placed in dishes of the sauce and then placed in the steamer to cook. If you have a single layered steamer, repeat the process in batches because overcrowding will result in under cooked fish. This recipe also works well with red snapper and mahi tuna.

4 fresh salmon steaks
2 shallots, finely minced
2 cloves garlic, finely minced
2 red Thai chilies, cut into small rounds, *(optional)*
2 Tbs. Thai Kitchen Premium Fish Sauce
2 Tbs. sugar
2 Tbs. fresh lime juice
1 tsp. freshly ground black pepper
1 cup fresh basil leaves

In a bowl, combine shallots, garlic, chilies, fish sauce, sugar, lime juice, pepper and basil leaves, mix well to combine. Place the fish in a 2 deep dish plates and cover with the sauce mixture.

Place a bamboo steamer over 2"-3" water in a wok or frying pan. Bring the water to a boil and carefully place the dishes in the steamer, being careful not to burn yourself on the steam. Cover and steam the fish for 7-10 minutes, or until it flakes easily with a fork. Remove the dishes carefully from the steamer and transfer the fish and sauce to a serving platter. Serves 4.

Shrimp and Roasted Red Chili Paste Stir-Fry (Nam Prik Pow)

This is a quick stir-fry that takes advantage of the fresh produce of summer.

2 Tbs. vegetable oil
2 tsp. garlic, finely chopped
½ cup yellow onion, coarsely chopped
1 tsp. brown sugar
1 Tbs. Thai Kitchen Roasted Red Chili Paste
2-3 Tbs. Thai Kitchen Premium Fish Sauce (or more to taste)
½ cup red bell pepper, cut into thin, ¼" strips
1 cup snow peas or sugar snap peas, left whole
12 oz. large shrimp, shelled and deveined

In a large wok or skillet, heat the vegetable oil over medium high heat. Add the garlic and onion and stir-fry for 30 seconds. Add the brown sugar, roasted red chili paste and fish sauce and continue stir-frying for 2-3 minutes, until the onion starts to wilt and soften. Add the peppers and peas and cook for 3 minutes. Add the shrimp and cook until the shrimp have turned orange-pink in color and are cooked through, about 1-2 minutes. Serves 2 to 3.

Deep Fried Whole Fish

Crisp and tasty. Thailand's version of a great Louisiana tradition.

> 1 whole fish (2 ½ to 3 lbs.) (red snapper, rock cod or
> your favorite fillets)
> 1 tsp. salt
> 1 tsp. cornstarch (or flour)
> 3 tsp. Thai Kitchen Premium Fish Sauce
> ¼ tsp. ginger powder
> ¼ tsp. garlic powder
> ¼ tsp. pepper
> 3 cups vegetable oil (for deep frying)
> Spicy Thai Gravy (page 119)
> *Optional garnish*: sprigs of fresh cilantro

Clean and scale fish. With a knife, make score marks across both sides of the fish.

In a bowl, combine salt, cornstarch, fish sauce, ginger powder, garlic powder, and pepper. Place fish in a shallow plate, evenly coat fish with mixture, and refrigerate for 1 hour. Turn and baste with dish juices occasionally.

Heat oil in a skillet or wok until hot. Deep fry each side until fish is golden brown and crisp. Place on a platter and pour Spicy Thai Gravy over the top. Serve with fresh cilantro sprigs on top. Serves 3 to 5.

Baked Tomato & Pineapple Fish

The original wrap! A banana leaf seals in juices and flavors.

1 whole rock cod (1 lb.) or any medium sized fish or fish fillet
1 whole banana leaf (or aluminum foil)
1 tsp. butter or margarine
1 cup chopped Chinese cabbage (or regular cabbage)
1 ½ Tbs. Thai Kitchen Premium Fish Sauce
1 Tbs. dry white wine
½ cup tomato sauce (or ¾ cup fresh tomatoes, diced)
½ cup pineapple pieces (fresh or canned)
1 small onion, thinly sliced
1 large tomato, thinly sliced
2 bell peppers, small, red or green, thinly sliced
1 tsp. sugar
1 tsp. pepper

Clean and scale fish. Lightly butter a (12" x 10") banana leaf.
Spread Chinese cabbage evenly across the bottom of the leaf.
Place fish in the center of the banana leaf over the cabbage.
Drizzle fish with fish sauce and wine and spread tomato sauce
evenly over the top of it. Cover fish with pineapple, onions,
tomatoes, bell peppers, sugar and sauce.

Tightly wrap the fish in the banana leaf, tie it down if necessary.
Place on a pan and bake at 350°F for 15-20 minutes. Serve with
your favorite sauce on the side. Serves 2 to 3.

Garlic Shrimp

Garlic lovers, here's your dish! Takes just a few minutes to prepare, for a simple and delicious stir-fry. Spear with toothpicks for an appetizer, or serve over jasmine rice as an entrée.

8-12 large shrimp (shelled and deveined)
2 Tbs. garlic, minced
½ Tbs. Thai Kitchen Premium Fish Sauce
1 tsp. pepper
1 ¼ tsp. sugar
4 Tbs. vegetable oil
4 sprigs of green onions, chopped
1 tsp. fresh ginger, thinly sliced
Optional garnish: sprigs of fresh cilantro

In a bowl, mix together shrimp, garlic, fish sauce, pepper and sugar. In a wok or skillet, heat oil over high heat until oil is hot. Add shrimp mixture into wok and stir-fry quickly until shrimp turn orange-pink in color, about 1-2 minutes. Add green onions and ginger. Stir-fry for an additional 30 seconds. Serve topped with fresh cilantro. Serves 2 to 3.

Steamed Fish with Broth *(Pla Pae Sa)*

Thai cooks know that steaming is the simple, healthful way to enhance the flavor and texture of fresh fish. Yet there's nothing bland about this dish, with its delicately spiced broth.

1 lb. fresh fish, whole or fillets
1-2 Tbs. vegetable oil
¼ cup fresh ginger, thinly sliced
2 cloves garlic, thinly sliced
2 cups chicken stock
3 Tbs. rice vinegar
2 tsp. sugar
Optional garnishes: sprigs of fresh cilantro, 2 stalks green onions,
       thinly sliced, 1 red chili, thinly sliced

Clean and scale fish. With a knife, make score marks on both sides. Place fish in a deep dish and drizzle oil over the top. Place ginger and garlic evenly over the top. Place dish in a steamer and steam on high for 8 minutes.

While fish is steaming, in a pot bring chicken stock, vinegar and sugar to a boil. Cook on high heat, stirring until sugar is dissolved. Pour this mixture over the fish and steam for an additional 3-5 minutes.

Remove fish from steamer and top with cilantro, green onions and red chili. Serve with your favorite sauce on the side. Serves 2 to 3.

Stuffed Squid with Shiitake Mushroom Sauce

The perfect combination of two Thai traditions: elaborate food presentation combined with their love of fresh seafood. This dish is tasty and beautiful.

6-8 whole squid, medium size
½ lb. pork, ground
1 tsp. fresh cilantro, chopped
¼ tsp. pepper
1 Tbs. garlic, minced
1 tsp. Thai Kitchen Premium Fish Sauce
1 tsp. sugar
1 Tbs. soy sauce
1 egg, lightly beaten
1 tsp. onion, finely chopped
Shiitake Mushroom Gravy (see recipe below)

Carefully clean squid, by removing the inside without puncturing the body. It is best to clean squid in the sink over some water as the purple dye can stain clothing and counters. Keep the body whole so that you can stuff and cook it without breaking. Set aside.

In a bowl, mix together pork, cilantro, pepper, garlic, fish sauce, sugar, soy sauce, egg and onion. Mix well so that all ingredients are well blended. With a small spoon or with your hands, carefully stuff this pork mixture into the squid. Place squid into a steamer and steam for 10-15 minutes. Remove squid and cut into 1-inch slices. You can serve squid at this time with your favorite dipping sauce or you can prepare it with the mushroom gravy. Serves 2 to 3.

Shiitake Mushroom Gravy:
¼ cup vegetable oil
1 tsp. garlic, minced
2 tsp. ginger, sliced
6-8 shiitake mushrooms*, medium size, softened and sliced
1 Tbs. Chinese oyster flavored sauce (or soy sauce)
3 stalks green onions, cut into 1-inch sections

In a pan, sauté oil, garlic and ginger on medium heat for 30 seconds until mixture is fragrant and garlic is slightly brown. Add mushrooms, oyster sauce and sliced steamed squid into the mixture. Sauté lightly, so that you do not break squid, for 4-5 minutes until sauce is evenly mixed. Add green onions and serve.

* See, Mushrooms, Shiitake, page 179.

Stuffed Crab Shells

Impress your friends and family members with the Thai tradition of elaborate food presentation. The use of crab shells will gain extra attention at your dinner table.

> 3 large whole crabs
> 1 cup ground pork
> ½ Tbs. fresh cilantro, chopped
> 1 Tbs. Thai Kitchen Premium Fish Sauce (or soy sauce)
> 1 tsp. garlic, minced
> ¼ tsp. pepper
> ½ tsp. salt
> 2 eggs
> 3 Tbs. breadcrumbs, fine
> 2 cups vegetable oil (for deep frying)
> *Optional garnishes:* sprigs of fresh cilantro and red chili, finely
> sliced

Wash crabs with water. Place crabs in a steamer and cook on high heat for 5-8 minutes. Remove meat from crab and place in a bowl, saving the large crab shell bodies. Mix crab meat with pork, cilantro, fish sauce, garlic, pepper, salt and 1 egg until all ingredients are blended together well. Stuff this mixture into the crab shells.

In a bowl, beat remaining 1 egg. With a spoon or a kitchen brush, place a thin layer of egg on top of the crab and pork stuffing in the exposed part of each crab shell. Top with bread crumbs. Heat oil in a large frying pan. Place the stuffed crabs in the oil with the exposed crab and pork mixture facing down into the oil. Fry for 3-5 minutes until bread crumbs turn a golden brown. Top with cilantro and chili and serve with your favorite sauce on the side. Serves 3.

NOTE: If whole crabs are not available, use store bought crab meat and oven proof cooking cups. Allow ½ cup of crab meat per crab in the recipe (for this recipe, you would need 1 ½ cups of crab meat). Follow instructions above and stuff meat into oven-proof cups. Top with egg and breadcrumbs. Steam for 10-15 minutes on high heat or bake at 350°F for 15 minutes. Remove from steamer or oven and allow to cool before removing from cups. Serve these crab cups topped with cilantro and chili and your favorite sauce on the side.

Basil Shrimp

Use any variety of fresh basil for this classic stir-fry. Don't even think of substituting dried basil – the delicate aromatic fragrance of the fresh herb is part of the appeal of this dish.

4 cloves garlic, minced
1 slice or piece fresh Chinese ginger
½ tsp. coarsely ground pepper
½ lb. large shrimp, shelled and deveined, tail on
1 Tbs. Thai Kitchen Premium Fish Sauce
1 cup fresh basil leaves
2 Tbs. vegetable oil
juice from ½ lime
Optional: 1 tsp. chili oil or 1 small chili, thinly sliced

In a wok, sauté garlic, ginger and pepper on high heat until fragrant and garlic begins to brown. Add shrimp and quickly stir-fry until shrimp turn orange-pink in color, about 1-2 minutes. Add fish sauce, basil leaves, optional chili oil. Stir-fry quickly until basil becomes limp. Remove from heat and squeeze lime juice over the top and serve. Makes 2 servings.

Vegetables

Vegetables are one of the glories of Thai cuisine. They grow in such variety and abundance that Thais are experts in their preparation. Vegetables are combined with fresh herbs and spices for subtle, complex flavors that are never boring or common. Prepared the Thai way, vegetables may become the favorite part of your meal.

Basic Vegetable Stir-Fry Recipe

This is a "skeleton" recipe, meaning use this as the basic idea for stir-fry but add your own embellishments for a special dish. Great as a side dish just as is.

3 cloves garlic, minced
2-3 Tbs. oil (for stir-frying)
2 Tbs. Thai Kitchen Roasted Red Chili Paste
12 oz. assorted vegetables (try zucchini, yellow squash,
      mushrooms)
1 tsp. brown sugar (optional)
1-2 Tbs. Thai Kitchen Premium Fish Sauce (or use soy sauce to
      make vegan)

In a wok or skillet, sauté garlic in hot oil until golden brown, being careful not to burn it. Add roasted red chili paste, mixed vegetables, sugar and fish sauce. Stir-fry until vegetables are cooked but still crisp. Makes 3 to 4 servings.

Roasted Eggplant with Tofu and Basil

A hearty, spicy main dish delight. This is nutritious tofu for people who thought they'd never like tofu.

> 1 lb. Japanese eggplants (about 4)
> 2 Tbs. Thai Kitchen Premium Fish Sauce
> 1 Tbs. brown sugar
> 1 Tbs. fresh lime juice
> 2 tsp. Thai Kitchen Spicy Thai Chili Sauce
> 1 Tbs. vegetable oil
> 1 Tbs. garlic, minced
> 2 small shallots, thinly sliced
> 8 oz. firm tofu, strained and cubed
> ¼ cup basil leaves, thinly sliced

Place eggplants on a lightly oiled baking sheet and broil 3" to 4" from heat until skin chars and blisters, rotating frequently, about 10 minutes. Let cool, then peel and slice diagonally ¼" thick. Combine fish sauce, brown sugar, lime juice and spicy Thai chili sauce; blend well. Heat oil in a wok or heavy skillet on medium-high. Add garlic and shallots and stir-fry until golden brown. Add eggplant and sauce mixture and cook 2 minutes, stirring frequently. Gently stir in tofu and basil; remove from heat, cover, and let stand 5 minutes to blend flavors. Makes 3 to 4 servings.

Tom Yum Stir-Fry

Tom Yum means hot and sour and that's a great description of this simple vegetable dish. Substitute your favorite vegetables if green beans aren't in season.

1 Tbs. vegetable oil
2 cloves garlic, finely minced
2 Tbs. Thai Kitchen Tom Yum Hot & Sour Soup Mix
2 Tbs. Thai Kitchen Premium Fish Sauce
1 Tbs. brown sugar
2 Tbs. fresh lime juice
3 cups Chinese long beans* or green beans, cut into 2" lengths
1 cup red bell pepper, cut into thin 1/8" strips

Heat a wok or large frying pan over medium high heat; add the vegetable oil and heat. Add the garlic, tom yum hot & sour soup mix, fish sauce, sugar and lime juice. Stir-fry for 1 minute, until the mixture becomes fragrant. Add the beans and mix well to combine. Cover the wok and let the beans cook for 3-5 minutes, stirring once or twice during cooking. Uncover, add the red pepper strips and cook for an additional 2 minutes. Serve immediately. Serves 2 to 3 as a main course and 4 as a side dish.

* Chinese long beans are widely used in Thai cuisine and many grocery stores now carry them.

Spicy Broccoli

This dish is gorgeous green and firecracker spicy. It's delicious served hot or cold. Enjoy it tossed into your salad bowl with crisp lettuce, cherry tomatoes and sweet red peppers.

> 1 Tbs. vegetable oil
> 4 cups broccoli florets
> ¼ cup vegetable broth or water
> ½ tsp. salt
> 2 Tbs. Thai Kitchen Red Chili Dipping Sauce

In a hot wok or skillet, heat vegetable oil for 1 minute over medium high heat and then add broccoli. Toss until bright green; add vegetable broth and cover tightly. Reduce heat to medium and cook 2 to 3 minutes, until tender crisp. Uncover and add salt and the red chili dipping sauce, toss well and transfer to a serving dish. Makes 3 to 4 servings.

Sweet & Sour Tofu Stir-Fry

Satisfying, light and colorful –- this is the gourmet way to eat vegetarian.

14 oz. firm tofu, strained and cut into ½" cubes
2 Tbs. soy sauce
2-4 cloves garlic, finely minced
1 1" piece fresh ginger, finely minced
1-2 Tbs. Thai Kitchen Spicy Thai Chili Sauce
1 Tbs. vegetable oil
1 medium sized onion, cut into ½" chunks
1 green bell pepper, cut into ½" chunks
1 red bell pepper, cut into ½" chunks
1 (8 oz.) small can pineapple pieces, drained
4-6 Tbs. Thai Kitchen Light Plum Spring Roll Sauce

While you are cutting up the vegetables, place the tofu in a small bowl with the soy sauce, garlic, ginger and spicy Thai chili sauce to marinate. Heat the oil in a large wok or skillet over medium high heat. Add the onion and stir-fry for 3 minutes. Add the tofu and stir-fry for 3-5 minutes. Add the green and red peppers, the pineapple and the light plum spring roll sauce and stir-fry for an additional 5 minutes. Serves 4.

Eggplant Satay

Try using zucchini or yellow squash as well! The prep time is cut short by broiling the eggplant without skewering it first.

3 cloves garlic
½ cup Thai Kitchen Pure Coconut Milk (Regular or Lite)
1 tsp. salt
2 tsp. Thai Kitchen Red Curry Paste
4-6 Japanese eggplants (the long, thin variety), cut into
      lengthwise strips ¼" thick
1 (8 oz.) jar Thai Kitchen Peanut Satay Sauce (Original Recipe or
      Spicy)

In a blender or food processor, purée garlic, coconut milk, salt and red curry paste. Place the eggplant in a shallow dish and cover with the marinade. Refrigerate 4 hours or overnight. Broil the eggplant for 2-3 minutes per side, until browned and cooked. Serve with Thai Kitchen Peanut Satay Sauce (Original Recipe or Spicy) on the side. Serves 2.

Veggie Kabobs

Try a variety of vegetables and grill them alongside Thai barbecued chicken or ribs.

4 long bamboo or metal skewers*
1 (14 oz.) can Thai Kitchen Pure Coconut Milk (Regular or Lite)
2 tsp. Thai Kitchen Red Curry Paste
1 Tbs. Thai Kitchen Premium Fish Sauce
1 cup medium sized mushrooms, washed and left whole
1 cup zucchini or summer squash, cut into 1" pieces
1 cup green or red bell pepper, cut into 1" pieces
1 cup onion, cut into large, 1" pieces
Optional: Thai Kitchen Red Chili Dipping Sauce

Marinade: In a bowl, combine the coconut milk, red curry paste and fish sauce. Set aside.

Skewer the vegetables, alternating the different varieties, place in a shallow dish and pour the marinade over the skewers. Marinate for 2-3 hours or overnight. Reserve the marinade from the dish and use as a baste during cooking. Place the skewers on a hot grill (or broil them). Baste with the marinade and grill for 20-30 minutes, (or broil for 5-7 minutes on each side) until the vegetables are browned and cooked through. Serve with Thai Kitchen Red Chili Dipping Sauce on the side for dipping.
Serves 4.

* If using bamboo skewers, soak them in water for ½ hour before making the kabobs so they won't burn on the grill.

Green Curry with Vegetables *(Keow Wan)*

A bright and colorful mix of vegetables makes this dish beautiful as well as savory.

1 (14 oz.) can Thai Kitchen Pure Coconut Milk (Regular or Lite)
1-4 Tbs. Thai Kitchen Green Curry Paste
1 cup vegetable stock or water
2 tsp. salt
2 Tbs. brown sugar
¼ cup basil leaves, chopped
2 cups assorted vegetables, cut into 1" pieces (try red bell pepper,
      zucchini, peas, or your favorite combination)
Thai Kitchen Jasmine Rice

Add the coconut milk, green curry paste, stock, salt, brown sugar and basil to a 2 quart saucepan and bring to a boil. Reduce heat to low and simmer for 15 minutes. Add the vegetables and simmer for an additional 5-10 minutes, until the vegetables are tender. Serve over cooked Thai Kitchen Jasmine Rice. Serves 4.

Tom Yum Corn Curry

Enjoy as a light entree, or as a spicy lift for broiled chicken or fish.

2 (14 oz.) cans Thai Kitchen Pure Coconut Milk (Regular or Lite)
2 Tbs. Thai Kitchen Tom Yum Hot & Sour Soup Mix
1 Tbs. Thai Kitchen Roasted Red Chili Paste
1 Tbs. Thai Kitchen Premium Fish Sauce
1 small bag frozen corn
3 cups asparagus or broccoli, cut into 1" pieces
Thai Kitchen Jasmine Rice
Optional garnish: lime wedges

In a 2 quart saucepan, mix the coconut milk with tom yum hot & sour soup mix, roasted red chili paste and fish sauce until well blended. Add the corn and simmer over medium heat for 10 minutes. Add the asparagus or broccoli and simmer for 5-7 minutes, until the vegetables are tender. Serve over cooked Thai Kitchen Jasmine Rice. Squeeze juice from a lime wedge over the curry. Serves 4.

Rice & Noodles

Rice is the major export crop of Thailand and a staple in the Thai diet, eaten at every meal. Thailand is world-famous for its jasmine rice. The recipes in this chapter use Thai Kitchen Jasmine Rice, a fragrant and naturally nutty rice grown in the fertile central plains of Thailand.

Noodle dishes are eaten like snacks, bought from street vendors and enjoyed on the run as well as in more formal settings. Rice noodles are made by blending rice flour and water into a light liquid paste, which is then extruded into thin paper-like sheets in the desired size, steam cooked and dried. Fresh rice noodles have a slightly different taste and texture. They would be equally delicious in these recipes and can now be found in many Asian markets. Best used the day you buy them.

Basic Thai Fried Rice Recipe

This is your "basic" fried rice. Add your favorite items to make it your own special creation. This recipe is perfect for left overs.

> 2 Tbs. vegetable oil (divided)
> 1 egg
> ½ cup of your favorite vegetables or ¼ lb. of your favorite meat
> 1 cup cooked Thai Kitchen Jasmine Rice* (cooled at least 1 hour
>   or leftover rice that has been refrigerated overnight)
> 1 tsp. sugar (optional)
> 1-1 ½ Tbs. Thai Kitchen Premium Fish Sauce

Add 1 Tbs. vegetable oil to a large skillet or wok, over a medium high flame; add the egg and cook until scrambled. Remove egg and set aside.

Add remaining 1 Tbs. oil to a large skillet or wok. Over medium-high heat, add your vegetable or meat. Stir-fry for 2-3 minutes until at least half way cooked. Add cooked jasmine rice, sugar and fish sauce. Stir-fry for an additional 2-3 minutes until all ingredients are cooked. Add egg; mix well until combined. Serves 2.

* See, Fried Rice, page 200.

Thai Fried Rice

The perfect treat for those who like their rice hot and spicy!

2 Tbs. vegetable oil (divided)
1 egg, beaten well
1 small yellow onion, chopped
1 clove garlic, finely minced
½ tsp. salt
1 tsp. brown sugar
3 cups cooked Thai Kitchen Jasmine Rice* (cooled at least 1 hour or leftover rice that has been refrigerated overnight)
2 Tbs. (or more) Thai Kitchen Spicy Thai Chili Sauce
½ cup mixed vegetables (try diced red bell peppers or frozen peas)
Optional: ¼ lb. small shrimp, shelled and deveined, or firm tofu, strained and cubed

Add 1 Tbs. vegetable oil to a large skillet or wok, swirling to coat the pan. Heat over a medium high flame, add the egg and cook until well scrambled. Remove egg and set aside.

Add remaining 1 Tbs. oil to the wok. Over medium high heat, stir-fry the onion, garlic, salt and brown sugar for 3-5 minutes, until the onion and garlic have just turned golden. Add cooked jasmine rice, spicy Thai chili sauce, vegetables and egg (and optional shrimp or tofu), stir-frying to combine. Stir-fry for an additional 2-3 minutes until all ingredients are cooked. Serve hot with more Thai Kitchen Spicy Thai Chili Sauce on the side for those who like added heat. Serves 2.

* See, Fried Rice, page 200.

Thai Rice Salad *(Khao Yam Pak)*

*This is a light and tasty salad that's perfect as a quick lunch or dinner.
Use leftover rice and cold barbecued chicken or ribs or sliced sandwich
meat.*

> 3 cups cooked Thai Kitchen Jasmine Rice
> 2 cups cooked chicken, pork (ham is delicious!) or beef, cut into
> small ½" pieces
> 1 cup red bell pepper, cut into small ¼" pieces
> 1 small can pineapple chunks
> *Optional garnish*: 4 whole lettuce leaves and chili peppers, finely
> chopped

> *Dressing*:
> 4 Tbs. Thai Kitchen Lemon Grass Salad Splash
> 1-2 Tbs. Thai Kitchen Premium Fish Sauce
> 2 Tbs. fresh lime juice
> 2 Tbs. vegetable oil
> 1 tsp. garlic, finely minced
> ¼ cup fresh cilantro, finely minced

Combine all ingredients in a jar and shake vigorously; set aside.

In a large salad bowl, combine the jasmine rice, meat, bell
pepper and pineapple chunks. Add the dressing. Toss well and
serve on lettuce leaves; garnish with chili peppers. Serves 4.

Sweet Pork Fried Rice

Chop up just a bit of leftover pork (we list a half cup, but you can add more) and have a hearty hot-and-sweet side dish or main course.

1 cup cooked Thai Kitchen Jasmine Rice
2 Tbs. vegetable oil, (divided)
½ cup chopped Sweet Pork (see page 44)
2 tsp. minced garlic
2 eggs, lightly beaten
1 tsp. thick Chinese soy sauce (optional)
2 Tbs. Thai Kitchen Premium Fish Sauce
¼ tsp. white pepper
2 Tbs. green onions, thinly sliced
Optional garnishes: sprigs of fresh cilantro and cucumber*, thinly sliced
Optional: Thai Kitchen Spicy Thai Chili Sauce

Heat 1 tablespoon of the oil in a wok or large skillet over medium-high heat. Stir-fry pork and garlic for 1 to 2 minutes or until light brown. Remove from wok and set aside. Add the remaining 1 tablespoon oil and coat bottom of wok. Add eggs and stir-fry for 30 seconds; until scrambled. Add cooked jasmine rice and stir-fry rapidly, turning jasmine rice over to coat with eggs. Add pork and garlic stir-fried mixture, soy sauce, fish sauce and white pepper; stir-fry for 1 minute. Add green onions and cook for 30 seconds more. Place on a serving platter or in a bowl and garnish with sprigs of fresh cilantro and sliced cucumber. Accompany with Thai Kitchen Spicy Thai Chili Sauce. Makes 4 to 6 servings.

* For a decorative touch, cut cucumbers in half lengthwise and then into thin half moon shapes. Fan cucumber on top of fried rice for garnish.

Coconut Rice

This is a very nice mild and creamy dish to serve with spicy meats and curries.

> 1 ½ cups Thai Kitchen Jasmine Rice
> 1 (14 oz.) can Thai Kitchen Pure Coconut Milk (Regular or Lite)
> 1 ¼ cups water
> 1 tsp. sugar
> pinch of salt
> *Optional garnishes*: toasted shredded coconut and chopped fresh
>   cilantro

Rinse jasmine rice with water and drain well. In a saucepan combine coconut milk, water, sugar and salt. Stir until sugar is dissolved and the ingredients are well blended. Stir in jasmine rice; mix well. Bring to a boil over medium heat. Cover tightly, reduce heat, and simmer 18 to 20 minutes. Check for doneness at end of cooking time and add a little more water if necessary and simmer for a few more minutes. Sprinkle with shredded coconut and chopped cilantro, if desired. Makes 4 to 6 servings.

Sweet Crispy Rice Noodles with Shrimp (Mee Krob)

Mee Krob is a special occasion dish and is served at every Thai feast. Every family has its own version of this dish and we think your whole family will enjoy our recipe. It takes slightly longer to prepare than the other dishes included here, but Mee Krob is always worth the wait!

1 (7 oz.) package Thai Kitchen Thin Rice Noodles
vegetable oil (for deep frying)
2 Tbs. vegetable oil for stir-frying
¼ lb. ground pork
¼ lb. shrimp, shelled and deveined
1 Tbs. garlic, finely minced
2 Tbs. chopped shallots
2 Tbs. Thai Kitchen Premium Fish Sauce
2 Tbs. rice vinegar
1 Tbs. Chinese oyster flavored sauce
1 red Thai chili pepper, finely minced
½ cup brown sugar
¼ cup fresh lime juice
2 cups fresh bean sprouts
Optional garnishes: 1 bunch green onions, cut diagonally into 2"
       lengths, lime wedges, sprigs of fresh cilantro, and thin-
       sliced red bell pepper

Note: Deep frying is a challenge and it is made easy by preparing your kitchen in advance. Start by choosing a large (4 quart or bigger) pan. You will also need 2 large slotted serving spoons to remove the noodles from the oil. The noodles need to drain on a few layers of paper towels -- try lining 2 cookie sheets with towels -- this will help absorb any excess oil. For deep frying, do not use olive oil! Plain vegetable oil is the best -- it won't impart any flavor to the noodles. Always use a thermometer to monitor the temperature of the oil and adjust the heat to keep the oil between 325°F and 350°F.

Break the rice noodles into small, fist sized clumps. Drop one small noodle into the oil. It should sizzle and rise to the top if the oil is ready. Add one clump of noodles to the oil. They will swell up and turn lightly golden in just a few seconds so keep your eyes on them at all times. Using the slotted spoons, remove the noodles and place on the paper towels to drain. Repeat this process until all of the noodles are cooked.

Heat 2 Tbs. vegetable oil in a wok or skillet. Add the ground pork and stir-fry for 2 minutes until the meat is no longer pink. Add the shrimp and continue to stir-fry another 2 minutes. Transfer the shrimp and pork from the wok to a small bowl and set aside. Add the garlic and shallots to the hot wok and stir-fry for 1 minute, being careful not to burn the garlic. The shallots will soften and the garlic will turn golden brown. Add the fish sauce, rice vinegar, oyster flavored sauce, chili pepper and sugar and bring to a boil, stirring well to dissolve the sugar. Continue to simmer the sauce for 7-10 minutes, until it begins to thicken. Add the lime juice and stir well. Add the reserved pork and shrimp mixture and stir well to coat. Add the deep fried rice noodles one batch at a time, mixing gently to avoid breaking the noodles. Once all of the noodles have been coated, turn them onto a large serving platter. Pile the bean sprouts to one side of the noodles. Decorate the platter with green onions, lime wedges, fresh cilantro and thin slices of red pepper. Serve warm or at room temperature. Serves 6 to 8.

Pad Thai Noodles - Quick & Easy Recipe

The classic dish when you crave the exotic flavors of Thailand but are pressed for time. We use a traditional Thai recipe that has been handed down from generation to generation so that you can enjoy authentic restaurant style Pad Thai Noodles quickly and easily in your own home.

4 oz. (approx. half package) Thai Kitchen Stir-Fry Rice Noodles*
3 Tbs. vegetable oil
1 egg, lightly beaten
4 oz. chicken, prawns or vegetables, sliced
½ jar (4 oz.) Thai Kitchen Pad Thai Sauce
4 oz. firm tofu, strained and cut into ½" cubes
½ cup bean sprouts
¼ cup unsalted peanuts, crushed
Optional garnish: sprigs of fresh cilantro, lime wedges, and
      chilies

Bring 2 cups of water to a boil (or use very hot tap water). Turn off heat and immerse rice noodles in hot water for 3-5 minutes until noodles are soft, cooked through but still firm and al dente, not mushy. (Check firmness frequently, as you would regular pasta.) Rinse with cold water for 30 seconds. Drain well and set aside.

Heat 1 Tbsp. vegetable oil in a wok or frying pan. Add egg and fry until scrambled. Remove and set aside. Heat 2 Tbsp. vegetable oil in a wok or frying pan. Add sliced chicken, prawns, or vegetables. Stir-fry for 1 minute. Add noodles, pad thai sauce and tofu. Stir-fry for 3-5 minutes or until all ingredients are well cooked. Add bean sprouts, peanuts and scrambled egg. Mix well to combine. Serve immediately with sprigs of cilantro, lime wedges, and fresh chilies. Serves 2.

* See, Rice Noodle Preparation, page 201.

Pad Thai Noodles - American Style

Authentic tasting Pad Thai Noodles are difficult to make outside of Thailand without authentic ingredients. Thai Kitchen has developed this recipe that closely resembles the real thing, using ingredients that can be easily found at your local supermarket.

> 1 pkg. (7 oz.) Thai Kitchen Stir-Fry Rice Noodles*
> 3 Tbs. sugar
> 1 Tbs. lime juice
> 2 ½ Tbs. Thai Kitchen Premium Fish Sauce
> 1 Tbs. rice vinegar
> 1 tsp. paprika (optional)
> 1 egg, well beaten
> 3 Tbs. vegetable oil
> 1 Tbs. garlic, minced
> 6 oz. chicken, prawns, vegetables or tofu, sliced
> 1 cup bean sprouts
> ½ cup unsalted peanuts, crushed
> *Optional garnishes*: sprigs of fresh cilantro, fresh chilies, and lime
>   wedges

Soak rice noodles in cold water for at least 1 hour (noodles can be soaked longer and even overnight). Drain all water and set aside.

In a bowl, combine sugar, lime juice, fish sauce, rice vinegar and paprika (optional). Set aside. Heat 1 Tbs. oil in a wok or frying pan; cook 1 well beaten egg until scrambled. Remove and set aside. In the same wok or frying pan, heat 2 Tbs. vegetable oil. Add chopped garlic and sliced chicken, prawns, vegetables or tofu. Stir-fry for 1 minute. Add pre-soaked, strained rice noodles and sauce mixture. Stir-fry for 3-5 minutes or until all ingredients are well cooked. Add bean sprouts, crushed peanuts and scrambled egg. Mix well to combine. Serve immediately with lime wedges, cilantro and fresh chilies. Serves 4.

* See, Rice Noodle Preparation, page 201.

Pad Thai Noodles – Traditional Recipe

Sweet, sour and salty tastes all blend and balance in this traditional Thai favorite. The fruity-sour taste of tamarind is almost impossible to duplicate, and is worth searching for in Asian or Indian markets.

1 pkg. (7 oz.) Thai Kitchen Stir-Fry Rice Noodles*
¼ cup tamarind juice*
1 ½ Tbs. Thai Kitchen Premium Fish Sauce
1 Tbs. rice vinegar
1 Tbs. sugar
½ tsp. paprika (optional)
2 Tbs. vegetable oil
1 Tbs. garlic, minced
6 shrimp, shelled and deveined
2 oz. tofu, cubed
1 egg, lightly beaten
½ cup bean sprouts
¼ cup unsalted peanuts, crushed
Optional garnishes: sprigs of fresh cilantro and lime wedges

Soak rice noodles in cold water for at least 1 hour (noodles can be soaked longer and even over night). Drain and set aside.

In a bowl, combine tamarind juice, fish sauce, rice vinegar, sugar, and paprika. Set aside. Heat oil in a wok, add garlic. Sauté for 30 seconds until garlic is fragrant. Add shrimp, tofu and egg. Stir-fry for 1 minute, until egg is scrambled. Add rice noodles and tamarind juice mixture. Stir-fry all ingredients until well cooked and combined. Serve with bean sprouts on the side, peanuts sprinkled over the top, with fresh cilantro and lime wedge garnishes. Serves 4.

* See, Rice Noodle Preparation, page 201.
* See, Tamarind, Juice/Paste, page 195.

Peanut Noodles

Nobody knows peanut sauces like Thai cooks. Here is one of their simplest and best noodle dishes. Serve warm or at room temperature, perfect anytime.

> 1 jar (8 oz.) Thai Kitchen Peanut Satay Sauce (Original Recipe or Spicy)
> 1 red bell pepper, cut into small strips ¼" wide and 1" long
> 1 cucumber, peeled and cut into small strips ¼" wide and 1" long
> 1 large carrot, grated coarsely
> ½ tsp. salt
> 1 tsp. sugar
> 1 (7 oz.) package Thai Kitchen Stir-Fry Rice Noodles
> *Optional garnishes*: sprigs of fresh cilantro and ¼ cup crushed unsalted peanuts

In a large bowl, combine the peanut satay sauce, bell pepper, cucumber, carrot, salt, and sugar in a large mixing bowl. Mix thoroughly and set aside.

Bring a large pot of water to a rolling boil. Add the noodles and cook for 3-5 minutes until noodles are soft, cooked through but still firm and al dente, not mushy. (Check firmness frequently, as you would regular pasta.) Rinse with cold water for 30 seconds. Drain water from the noodles and immediately add the warm noodles to the vegetable mixture. Toss well to combine and garnish with cilantro and chopped peanuts. Serves 2 to 3 as a meal and 4 as a side dish.

Wide Noodles with Gravy and Broccoli (Lad Nah)

This traditional Thai dish is a great way to serve broccoli -- a low-fat gravy with a hearty taste.

1 (7 oz.) package Thai Kitchen Wide-Style Rice Noodles*
1 Tbs. vegetable oil (divided)
2-3 Tbs. Chinese oyster flavored sauce or soy sauce (divided)
1 Tbs. chopped garlic
1 ½ cups broccoli, cut into 1" pieces
2 tsp. brown sugar
1 Tbs. cornstarch with 1 Tbs. cold water
1 ½ cups fat-free or low-fat beef, chicken or vegetable stock

Bring 2 cups of water to a boil (or use very hot tap water). Turn off heat and immerse rice noodles in hot water for 3-5 minutes until noodles are soft, cooked through but still firm and al dente, not mushy. (Check firmness frequently, as you would regular pasta.) Rinse with cold water for 30 seconds. Drain well and set aside.

In a large wok or skillet, heat ½ Tbs. oil. Add the noodles and 1 Tbs. oyster flavored sauce. Stir-fry for 2-3 minutes over medium high heat, until the noodles are evenly coated and glossy. Remove to a large serving platter. Add the remaining ½ Tbs. oil to the wok and the garlic. Stir-fry for 1 minute. Add the broccoli, remaining oyster sauce and sugar. Stir-fry for 2-3 minutes. In a small dish, add 1 Tbs. cold water to the cornstarch and mix well to dissolve. Be sure the mixture is smooth and there are no lumps. Add the stock and cornstarch mixture to the wok and continue to cook for 5-7 minutes, until the gravy begins to thicken. Pour the broccoli and gravy over the noodles and serve immediately. Serves 2 to 3 as a main course and 4 as a side dish.

* See, Rice Noodle Preparation, page 201.

Rice Noodles with Thai Pesto *(Pad Ka Pao)*

The flavors in this dish pack a mouthwatering punch. Thais traditionally use a mortar and pestle to make this sauce, but a blender or processor works just as well.

½ cup fresh cilantro
½ cup fresh basil
1 Tbs. garlic
1 Tbs. minced fresh galangal (Thai ginger) or Chinese ginger
1 Tbs. Thai Kitchen Spicy Thai Chili Sauce
¼ cup vegetable oil
1 tsp. salt
2 tsp. sugar
1 Tbs. fresh lime juice
4 oz. (approx. half package) Thai Kitchen Thin Rice Noodles

In a blender or food processor, purée the cilantro, basil, garlic, ginger, spicy Thai chili sauce, vegetable oil, salt, sugar and lime juice. Scrape down the sides and process until smooth.

Bring a large pot of water to a rolling boil. Add the noodles and cook for 3-5 minutes until noodles are soft, cooked through but still firm and al dente, not mushy. (Check firmness frequently, as you would regular pasta.) Drain water from the noodles. Immediately place the warm noodles in a serving bowl and toss with the pesto mixture. Serves 2.

Thai Sesame Noodles

Sesame seeds add taste and texture to vegetables and tofu, also making for a beautiful presentation.

2 Tbs. vegetable oil
2-3 cloves garlic, finely minced
2 cups asparagus (or broccoli florets), cut into 2" pieces
1 red bell pepper, sliced into ¼" strips
2 Tbs. water
4 oz. firm tofu, strained and cut into ½" cubes
1 Tbs. sesame oil
2-3 Tbs. soy sauce (or more to taste)
2-3 Tbs. Thai Kitchen Spicy Thai Chili Sauce (or more to taste)
3 Tbs. sesame seeds
1 (7 oz.) package Thai Kitchen Stir-Fry Rice Noodles

Heat the vegetable oil in a wok or large skillet over medium heat and sauté the garlic until golden, about 2-3 minutes. Add the asparagus and red bell pepper and stir-fry for 2-3 minutes. Add the water, cover and simmer for 5-7 minutes, until the vegetables are tender. While they cook, bring a large pot of water to a boil for the noodles. To the asparagus and bell pepper mixture, add the tofu, sesame oil, soy sauce, chili sauce and sesame seeds; mix well and remove from the heat.

Bring a large pot of water to a rolling boil. Add the noodles and cook for 3-5 minutes until noodles are soft, cooked through but still firm and al dente, not mushy. (Check firmness frequently, as you would regular pasta.) Drain water from the noodles. Place the warm noodles in a serving bowl and immediately toss with the asparagus mixture. Serve immediately. Serves 3 to 4.

Carrot & Cabbage Noodles

Noodles and vegetables are combined in a garden-fresh mix that's a side dish with chicken or beef, or a vegetarian meal.

> 1 (7 oz.) package Thai Kitchen Rice Noodles* (Stir-Fry, Thin or Wide-Style)
> 3 Tbs. peanut oil
> 2 Tbs. garlic, finely minced
> ½ cup red onion, finely chopped
> 2 tsp. brown sugar
> ½ cup carrots, coarsely grated
> 1 cup green cabbage, coarsely chopped
> 2 Tbs. Thai Kitchen Spicy Thai Chili Sauce
> 2 Tbs. soy sauce
> *Optional*: Thai Kitchen Red Chili Dipping Sauce

Bring 2 cups of water to a boil (or use very hot tap water). Turn off heat and immerse rice noodles in hot water for 3-5 minutes until noodles are soft, cooked through but still firm and al dente, not mushy. (Check firmness frequently, as you would regular pasta.) Rinse with cold water for 30 seconds. Drain well and set aside.

Heat the oil in a large wok or skillet over medium high heat and add the garlic. Stir-fry for 1 minute. Add the onion and brown sugar and stir-fry for 2-3 minutes, until the onion is soft. Add the carrots, cabbage, chili sauce and soy sauce and stir-fry for 5 minutes. Add the noodles, mix well and stir-fry for an additional 3-5 minutes. Serve immediately with red chili dipping sauce on the side. Serves 3 to 4.

* See, Rice Noodle Preparation, page 201.

Sweet & Spicy Noodles

Garnish each plate with a whole lettuce leaf.

> 1 Tbs. vegetable oil
> 1 lb. ground turkey, ground pork or chicken
> 1 (7 oz.) package Thai Kitchen Thin Rice Noodles
> ½ bunch fresh cilantro, finely chopped
> ½ bunch fresh mint, finely chopped
> 6-8 Tbs. Thai Kitchen Red Chili Dipping Sauce

Heat the vegetable oil in a large skillet and add the ground meat. Cook 3-5 minutes over high heat, until meat is thoroughly cooked and well browned. Drain the meat and place in a large salad bowl.

Bring a large pot of water to a rolling boil. Add the noodles and cook for 3-5 minutes until noodles are soft, cooked through but still firm and al dente, not mushy. (Check firmness frequently, as you would regular pasta.) Drain water from the noodles and immediately add the warm noodles to the meat.

Add the cilantro, mint and red chili dipping sauce and toss well to combine. Serve warm or at room temperature. Serves 4 to 6.

Sauces & Dips

The Thais enhance their meals with sauces and dips. It is typical to find an assortment of them collected on the table at one time. The flavors range from sweet and tangy to hot and spicy, from subtle to complex. Sauces allow diners to adjust the taste of a dish to their own liking. These delicious flavors are unique, yet quite simple to prepare.

Thai Table Sauce

You will find this flavorful dipping sauce served at the table in every Thai home!

    2 shallots, sliced into very thin rings
    1 red Thai chili pepper, thinly sliced
    1 Tbs. Thai Kitchen Premium Fish Sauce
    1 Tbs. fresh lime juice
    2 tsp. sugar

Combine ingredients and serve with your grilled meats or on the side with any savory Thai dish.

Eggplant Dipping Sauce

An ideal dipping sauce to serve with a platter of raw or lightly cooked vegetables.

6 cups water
1 tsp. salt
¾ lb. Japanese eggplant (about 3 medium sized)
1 lime, juice and rind
1 shallot, sliced
2 cloves garlic, crushed
3 Tbs. Thai Kitchen Red Chili Dipping Sauce

In a large saucepan, combine water and salt and bring to a boil. Peel eggplant and dice. Drop immediately into boiling water and cook for 8 minutes or until tender. Drain.

Squeeze the juice out of the lime. Save the rind and grate 1 tsp. of lime zest. In a food processor or blender, process eggplant, lime zest, lime juice, shallot, garlic and red chili dipping sauce until smooth. Season to taste with additional lime juice or salt. Serve with a variety of fresh or lightly cooked vegetables. Makes 1 cup.

Fiery Thai Salsa

Hot, sweet and spicy – spoon this salsa over simple grilled fish or chicken. Or, have you ever tried a Thai taco!

> 1 large ripe mango, peeled and seeded
> 1 small shallot, chopped
> ¼ cup fresh basil, coarsely chopped
> 2 cloves garlic, minced
> 2 Tbs. fresh lime juice
> 2 Tbs. Thai Kitchen Red Chili Dipping Sauce
> salt and coarsely crushed black pepper to taste

Coarsely chop mango. In a large bowl combine mango, shallot, basil, garlic and lime juice; mix well. Stir in red chili dipping sauce. Season to taste with salt and pepper. Makes 1 cup.

Vegetable Dip

A creamy dip with a spicy kick. Serve this to liven up your favorite chips or raw vegetables.

½ cup cream cheese
½ cup mayonnaise
½ cup sour cream
1 clove garlic, finely minced
1-2 Tbs. Thai Kitchen Spicy Thai Chili Sauce (or more to taste)
3 Tbs. chopped green onion

Combine the cream cheese, mayonnaise, and sour cream and beat until smooth. Add the garlic, spicy Thai chili sauce and green onion and mix well. Refrigerate for 3 hours before serving. Makes 1 ¾ cups

Cucumber Relish

Crunchy, pleasantly cool and sweet – the perfect condiment or topping.

1/3 cup rice vinegar
2 Tbs. sugar
1 tsp. salt
4 cucumbers, peeled and seeded, thinly sliced
2 shallots (or red onion), thinly sliced
Optional: 1 small chili, thinly sliced, and chopped fresh cilantro

In a small pot, heat vinegar, sugar and salt. Stir over low heat until sugar is dissolved. Let mixture cool.

In a bowl, combine cucumbers, shallots, chili and cooled vinegar mixture. Toss all ingredients together. Serve at room temperature or chill in the refrigerator, covered with plastic wrap for an hour, before serving. Makes 1 to 1 ½ cups.

Quick Peanut Satay Sauce

Here's help for those of you addicted to Thai Kitchen Peanut Satay Sauce. In a culinary crisis, use peanut butter from your cupboard for a close cousin to the real thing.

¾ cup creamy peanut butter
1-2 Tbs. Thai Kitchen Red Curry Paste
1 (14 oz.) can Thai Kitchen Pure Coconut Milk (Regular or Lite)
2-3 Tbs. sugar (to taste)
¼ cup unsalted roasted peanuts, crushed
Thai Kitchen Premium Fish Sauce or salt (to taste)
Optional: ¼ cup fresh whipping cream

In a bowl, mix together peanut butter and red curry paste. Mix well until evenly blended. In a wok or small pot, heat coconut milk on low heat until it begins to simmer. Add peanut butter and red curry paste mixture, and sugar. (For a thicker and creamier sauce, add fresh cream.) Simmer on low heat, stirring constantly, until sauce is well blended and begins to thicken. Add crushed peanuts, fish sauce (or salt) and cook for an additional minute.

Sweet Chili Sauce

A sweet-and-hot sauce to use in place of salsa or catsup. A provocative pick-me-up with fried fish, roasted meats, or scrambled eggs.

1 Tbs. fresh red chili, minced
½ cup rice vinegar
1 tsp. salt
1 Tbs. sugar
1 tsp. garlic, minced

In a small pot, heat chili, vinegar, salt, sugar and garlic together over low heat. Stir constantly until mixture thickens to a syrupy consistency. Makes 5 servings.

Peanut Gravy Sauce

An unusually rich and creamy gravy with spicy undertones. Serve over slices of roast turkey, or with any dish that takes a brown gravy.

1 (14 oz.) can Thai Kitchen Pure Coconut Milk (Regular or Lite)
2-3 Tbs. Thai Kitchen Red Curry Paste
1/3 cup chicken stock
2 ½ Tbs. Thai Kitchen Premium Fish Sauce
¾ cup unsalted roasted peanuts, crushed
3 Tbs. sugar
¼ tsp. salt
4-6 kaffir lime leaves*
¼ tsp. cornstarch (dissolved with 1 tsp. water)
Optional: ½ cup basil leaves (whole or chopped), 1 fresh red
　　　chili, thinly sliced

In a pot, mix coconut milk and red curry paste. Cook on low heat, stirring constantly, until red curry is evenly dissolved and mixture begins to simmer. Add chicken stock, fish sauce, peanuts, sugar, salt, kaffir lime leaves and cornstarch mixture. Bring all ingredients to a simmer stirring constantly until mixture begins to thicken slightly. Remove from heat and stir in fresh basil leaves and red chilies.

* Kaffir lime leaves are optional in this recipe. See, Kaffir Lime Leaves, page 193.

Spicy Pork & Tomato Dip

Serve on the side with your favorite Thai dish, with vegetables, or as a dip for chips.

1 cup cherry tomatoes
2-5 dried red chilies, soaked
1 Tbs. galangal (or fresh ginger), minced
3 Tbs. onion, minced
5 garlic cloves, whole
1 Tbs. Thai Kitchen Premium Fish Sauce*
2 Tbs. vegetable oil
2 garlic cloves, minced
4 Tbs. pork*, chopped
¼ cup fresh cilantro, chopped
½ cup water

In a blender, pulse tomatoes, chilies, galangal, onions, whole garlic cloves, and fish sauce until well blended and slightly chunky.

In a wok, add oil and sauté garlic until fragrant and slightly brown. Add pork and sauté for an additional 1-2 minutes until pork is cooked. Add tomato mixture and water. Stir-fry on low heat until all ingredients are mixed well and the sauce begins to simmer. Cook until mixture is reduced, the water has evaporated, and sauce is slightly thick.

Remove from heat, transfer to a bowl and stir in chopped cilantro. Makes 1 to 1 ½ cups.

* To make vegetarian, substitute fish sauce with soy sauce and prepare without pork.

Spicy Soy Sauce

The perfect mildly-spicy, everyday condiment. Ideal for barbecued meats.

2-4 fresh serrano chilies, minced, with or without seeds
¼ cup soy sauce
2 cloves garlic, minced
1 medium shallot (or onion), minced or thinly sliced
1 Tbs. fresh lime juice

In small bowl, combine chilies, soy sauce, garlic, shallot, and lime juice. Mix well.

Spicy Thai Gravy

This thick sauce is versatile. Serve on the side as a gravy or to pour over your fish or grilled meats.

3 Tbs. vegetable oil
1 Tbs. fresh galangal (or Chinese ginger), minced
1 small onion, chopped
2-4 serrano chilies, chopped (with or without seeds)
3 cloves garlic, minced
2 Tbs. soy sauce
2 Tbs. Thai Kitchen Premium Fish Sauce
1 Tbs. brown sugar
2 Tbs. rice vinegar
2 sprigs green onion, chopped
¼ cup flour, mixed with 1 ½ cups water until smooth
2 Tbs. fresh cilantro, chopped

In a pot or wok, add vegetable oil, galangal, onion, chilies, and garlic. Over medium heat, sauté ingredients until they become fragrant and garlic is browned. Add soy sauce, fish sauce, sugar, vinegar, green onions, flour and water mixture. Heat, stirring constantly, until sauce is well blended and begins to simmer. Remove from heat and stir in cilantro. Makes 1 ½ to 2 cups of sauce.

Beverages

In Thailand, with hot, sticky weather that can wilt you in seconds, everyone revives with a variety of beverages, day and night. Just as we quench a thirst with soda pop – Thais quench their thirsts with the natural nectars and exotic treats from mother nature. Fruit smoothies, luscious coconut drinks or combinations of juices are available fresh everywhere for a nice tropical refresher.

Lemon Grass Tea

A light and refreshing accompaniment to the complex flavors of Thai cuisine.

> 2 tsp. Thai Kitchen Lemon Grass (Dried) or 4 pieces fresh lemon grass*, cut in half and bruised
> 1 Tbs. fresh ginger, sliced or coarsely chopped
> 1 Tbs. honey (or more to taste)
> 2 cups boiling water
> *Optional garnish*: 2 sprigs of fresh mint

Combine lemon grass, ginger, honey and water in a tea pot. Bring to a boil for 5 minutes. Strain mixture through a coffee filter or a fine strainer to remove the lemon grass and ginger. Serve warm or cold with additional honey to taste. Decorate the cup with mint sprigs or add them to the tea for flavor. Serves 2.

* See, Lemon Grass, pages 194, 199.

Thai-Style Pina Colada

The ultmate tropical drink! Just find a palm tree and enjoy.

4 oz. Thai Kitchen Pure Coconut Milk (Regular or Lite)
4 oz. pineapple juice
4 oz. crushed ice
Optional: 2 oz. dark rum

In a blender, combine coconut milk, pineapple juice, ice and rum.
Blend until smooth. Serves 1.

Thai Banana Smoothie

It's a breakfast drink, it's a snack, it's a party beverage.

4 oz. Thai Kitchen Pure Coconut Milk (Regular or Lite)
4 oz. pineapple or orange juice
1 ripe banana
4 oz. ice

Combine the coconut milk, pineapple or orange juice, banana and ice in a blender and pulse until smooth. Serves 1.

Thai Summer Breeze

Try this delicious drink blended!

> 2 oz. Thai Kitchen Pure Coconut Milk (Regular or Lite)
> 2 oz. pineapple juice
> 2 oz. orange juice
> *Optional:* 2 oz. dark rum
> 4 oz. crushed ice
>
> Combine coconut milk, pineapple juice, orange juice and rum; blend until frothy, and serve over crushed ice. Serves 1.

Thai Iced Tea *(Cha Yen)*

Condensed milk is the key ingredient in this surprisingly simple drink.

2 Tbs. Thai Kitchen Thai Iced Tea (tea leaves) or black tea
1 cup water (or less for a richer taste)
4 Tbs. sugar
¼ cup condensed milk, unsweetened
crushed ice or ice cubes
Optional: 1 Tbs. milk, fresh cream or soy milk

Prepare Thai Kitchen Thai Iced Tea with hot water to desired taste. Strain tea leaves with a filter. In a cup, blend warm tea with sugar and condensed milk. Stir well until sugar is dissolved. Pour mixture into a tall glass filled with crushed ice. Top with optional milk, fresh cream or soy milk. Makes 2 servings.

NOTE: You can replace the sugar and unsweetened condensed milk with ¼ cup sweetened condensed milk.

Thai Iced Coffee *(Kafae Yen)*

Thais have been enjoying this refreshing drink for years. The taste is similar to an iced cafe mocha.

2 Tbs. ground coffee
1 cup water (or less for a richer taste)
4 Tbs. sugar
¼ cup condensed milk, unsweetened
crushed ice or ice cubes
Optional: 1 Tbs. milk, fresh cream or soy milk

Prepare coffee with hot water to desired taste. In a cup, blend warm coffee with sugar and condensed milk. Stir well until sugar is dissolved. Pour mixture into a tall glass filled with crushed ice. Top with optional milk, fresh cream or soy milk. Makes 2 servings.

NOTE: You can replace the sugar and unsweetened condensed milk with ¼ cup sweetened condensed milk.

Desserts

Thais love their sweets, from a simple fruit salad, to a baked custard, to a grilled banana sold by a street vendor. They incorporate the natural sweetness from fresh fruits in most of their desserts. The richly tropical flavor of coconut is always used in some form. We have included some of the most traditional Thai recipes as well as a few modern updates. And nothing cools the lingering heat of chilies better than a cool dessert.

Thai Tapioca Pudding

This is comfort food – but more exotic than your mother used to make.

½ cup small pearl tapioca
1 ½ cups water
1 (14 oz.) can Thai Kitchen Pure Coconut Milk (Regular or Lite)
1/3 cup sugar
1/8 tsp. salt
Optional: sliced mango, or peeled and seeded lychees

Place pearl tapioca in a sieve or strainer and rinse quickly under running cold water for 15-20 seconds. Bring water to a boil. Stir in tapioca. Reduce heat to medium and cook for about 10 to 12 minutes or until tapioca becomes translucent. Stir frequently to prevent tapioca from sticking to the bottom of the pan. Stir in coconut milk, sugar and salt. Simmer for 5 to 7 minutes, stirring frequently, until pudding becomes slightly thickened. Let cool for 20 minutes. Serve warm or cold. Top with sliced mango or lychees. Makes 4 to 6 servings.

Thai Bananas in Coconut Milk

Such an easy dessert and a great way to use over-ripe bananas!

> 1 (14 oz.) can Thai Kitchen Pure Coconut Milk (Regular or Lite)
> 3 large bananas, sliced into ½" slices
> 3 Tbs. brown sugar
> 1 tsp. vanilla
> pinch of salt

> In a pot, simmer all of the ingredients on low temperature for 10 minutes and serve warm. Serves 4.

Thai Coconut Pudding

Creamy and smooth – serve this coconut custard to balance a spicy Thai meal.

½ cup flour
½ cup sugar
pinch of salt
6 egg yolks
3 (14 oz.) cans Thai Kitchen Pure Coconut Milk (Regular or Lite)

Mix the flour, sugar and salt in a heavy bottomed saucepan. Add the egg yolks and whisk the mixture together -- it will be very thick. Slowly whisk in half a can of coconut milk and place over medium heat. Heat the mixture for 2-3 minutes, stirring constantly. In a small saucepan, heat and simmer the remaining coconut milk. Slowly add the hot coconut milk to the flour and egg mixture, whisking to combine. If the pudding is lumpy, don't worry -- continue to whisk. Simmer the mixture for 7-10 minutes, until it becomes very thick. Remove from the heat and place in a decorative serving bowl. This pudding is delicious served warm! Makes 10 to 12 servings.

Sticky Rice with Coconut and Mango

Mango is a delicious tropical fruit that has become more commonly available in the last few years. Here is a great trick for removing the meat. Cut the mango away from its center in 2 large halves. (The fruit around the center pit is quite hard and won't be used) Hold the mango with the skin down in the palm of your hand and with a sharp paring knife cut the flesh into 6 lengthwise strips then 6 crosswise strips. You can then cut away the meat from the skin into perfect chunks for Sticky Rice with Mango. Allow 1 ripe mango per person.

4-6 ripe mangoes
1 (14 oz.) can Thai Kitchen Pure Coconut Milk (Regular or Lite)
1 cup sugar
1 tsp. salt.
2 cups uncooked sticky rice* (makes about 5 cups, cooked)

Start by soaking 2 cups of sticky rice in cold water for 3 hours. Drain the rice and place in a medium shallow dish. Bring water in a steamer to a boil. Place dish in the steamer and cover with lid. Steam rice for 30-40 minutes.

Combine the coconut milk, sugar and salt in a small saucepan and simmer until the sugar has dissolved. Remove the coconut milk mixture from the heat and set aside.

As soon as the rice is cooked, put rice into a large bowl and pour the coconut mixture over it. Stir well to combine and let the rice rest for 30 minutes to an hour to absorb the coconut milk. You may serve the sticky rice on a serving platter or in individual bowls. Garnish platter or each bowl with the cut mango and enjoy warm or at room temperature. Serves 4 to 6.

* See, Cooking Sticky Rice, page 200.

Coconut Corn Pudding

Serve as a sweet and satisfying dessert, or as a mild side dish with spicy entrees.

3 cups corn, whole kernels (fresh, frozen or canned)
1 cup sugar
4 Tbs. tapioca flour (or corn flour)
1 cup Thai Kitchen Pure Coconut Milk (Regular or Lite)
½ tsp. salt
2 cups water

In a pot, bring water to a boil. Add corn and cook until it is tender, about 5 minutes. Add sugar and flour and cook until flour is well blended and sugar is dissolved. Add coconut milk and salt and bring to a boil, constantly stirring. Remove from heat and spoon into individual dessert cups. Serve warm or cold. Makes 4 servings.

Fusion Recipes

The Bay Area, home of Thai Kitchen, is a melting pot of Asian and Western cultures. The influences of this blending of cultures are quite evident on the menus of local restaurants. Bay Area chef Peter Moore has captured this unique combination of flavors for Thai Kitchen.

Crab & Shiitake Spring Rolls with Peanut Carrot Sauce

Once you've made a few, spring rolls are a snap, and an impressive and tasty appetizer. The filling on this one is relatively traditional, but you can really have fun thinking up new fillings. Duck, pomegranate and rice made a delicious combination.

2 Tbs. peanut oil
2 cups shiitake mushrooms*, thinly sliced
1 cup leek, diced
¼ cup water chestnuts, finely diced (apple or jicama may be
        substituted)
¼ cup Thai Kitchen Pure Coconut Milk (Regular or Lite)
¼ lb. fresh crab meat
¼ cup fresh cilantro, chopped
16 rice paper wrappers**
egg wash (1 large whole egg, mixed well with 2 Tbs. water)
peanut oil (for deep frying)
Peanut Carrot Sauce (see page 143)

In a wok or skillet, heat the 2 Tbs. oil over medium-high heat and lightly sauté mushrooms, leeks and water chestnuts for 3 to 4 minutes. Stir in coconut milk and cook for another 2 to 3 minutes. Allow the mushroom mixture to cool. In a bowl, combine this sauté mixture with crab meat and cilantro; mix well.

Preparation area: A bowl of warm water, a large shallow plate, moist towels, egg wash in a small bowl, a smooth flat surface. Be sure to remove as much excess liquid from the filling mixture as possible. With your hands, you may want to squeeze the mixture to remove any moisture.

Fill a large shallow plate with warm water. Dip a sheet of rice paper into warm water for 10–20 seconds to soften. Be sure the rice paper is full immersed in the water so that it will soften. Remove rice paper and lay it on a flat surface.

Place two Tbs. of filling in the center of each wrapper. Fold the bottom edge of the wrapper nearest you over this mound. Then, fold in both sides of the wrapper over the mound. Gently, roll the spring roll wrapper tightly away from you, until it has almost reached the top edge. Be careful not to break the fragile rice paper. Seal the edge with the egg wash. Repeat this process until you are finished with the filling. As you finish assembling the rolls, store them under damp towels so that they will not dry and turn hard.

In a wok or skillet, heat 2" of peanut oil to 350°F. Fry rolls for 3 to 5 minutes, turning them occasionally until golden brown. Watch them continuously so that they do not burn. You can fry more than one at a time.

Remove from oil and drain on absorbent paper towels. Serve with Peanut Carrot Sauce. Makes 12 to 14 spring rolls.

NOTE: If fresh crab meat is not available, you can use canned crab meat.

* See, Mushrooms, Shiitake, page 179.
** The recipe filling is for approximatley 12 to 14 rolls. Since some of the wrappers may break during rolling, we suggest you have extra available. Eggroll wrappers or spring roll wrappers can be substitued. See, Rice Paper Wrappers, page 181.

Shrimp, Proscuitto & Papaya Spring Rolls with Spicy Cucumber Sauce

These cold spring rolls make a terrific summer appetizer on a hot day. This recipe falls on the decidedly untraditional, but guests find them addictive.

1 ½ cups small cooked shrimp, shelled and deveined
1 ½ cups ripe papaya, diced
1 cup water chestnuts, diced (apple or jicama may be substituted)
2 tsp. lime juice
1 tsp. lemon grass*, minced
1 tsp. ginger, minced
1 to 2 Thai chilies, seeded and minced
16 round rice paper wrappers (9")**
10 paper-thin slices of proscuitto ham
Spicy Cucumber Sauce (see page 144) or Cucumber Relish (see
        page 113)

In a bowl, combine shrimp, papaya, water chestnuts, lime juice, lemon grass, ginger and chilies; toss lightly to mix.

Preparation area: A bowl of warm water, a large shallow plate, moist towels, a smooth flat surface.

Fill a large shallow plate with warm water. Dip a sheet of rice paper into the water for 10–20 seconds to soften. Be sure the rice paper is full immersed in water so that it will soften. Remove rice paper and lay it on a flat surface.

Top the wrapper with a slice of proscuitto. Place 2 Tbs. of filling along the bottom third of the wrapper. Fold the bottom edge of the wrapper nearest you over this mound. Gently, roll the spring roll wrapper tightly away from you, until it has reached the middle of the wrapper. Then, fold in both sides of the wrapper over this mound. Be careful not to break the fragile rice paper. Repeat this process until you are finished with the filling. As you finish assembling the rolls, store them under damp towels so that they will not dry and turn hard. It is not neccessary to fry these spring rolls as they are now ready to eat.

To serve, slice completed spring rolls on the diagonal and accompany with Spicy Cucumber Sauce or Cucumber Relish. Makes 10 spring rolls.

* Lemon grass is optional in this recipe. We recommend the use of fresh lemon grass only. Do not used dried. See, Lemon Grass, pages 194, 199.
** The recipe filling is for approximatley 10 rolls. Since some of the wrappers may break during rolling, we suggest you have extra available. See, Rice Paper Wrappers, page 181.

Peanut Carrot Sauce

Combining sweet, spicy and sour tastes with the crunchy textures of carrots and peanuts, this sauce makes a perfect accompaniment to spring rolls or even fried yams.

¼ cup rice vinegar
¼ cup fresh lime juice
2 Tbs. Thai Kitchen Premium Fish Sauce
1 Tbs. palm sugar or brown sugar
1 tsp. garlic, minced
½ tsp. Thai Kitchen Spicy Thai Chili Sauce or
      2 Thai chilies, seeds removed and minced
½ cup carrot, grated
¼ cup roasted unsalted peanuts, coarsely chopped

In a bowl, combine vinegar, lime juice, fish sauce, palm sugar, garlic and spicy Thai chili sauce; mix well. Chill for at least an hour. Sprinkle with carrot and chopped peanuts before serving. Makes approximately 1 – 1 ½ cups of sauce.

Spicy Cucumber Sauce

This sauce has a sharp clean flavor that complements hot or cold spring rolls, as well as fish cakes.

> 2 Tbs. Thai Kitchen Lemon Grass Salad Splash
> 2 Tbs. rice vinegar
> 2 Tbs. water
> ½ tsp. Thai Kitchen Spicy Thai Chili Sauce or
>   1 Thai chili, seeded and thinly sliced
> ½ cup cucumber, thinly sliced
> *Optional garnish*: fresh cilantro leaves

In a bowl, combine lemon grass salad splash, vinegar, water and spicy Thai chili sauce; blend well. Pour mixture over cucumber slices. Marinate in the refrigerator for at least 1 hour. Top with cilantro leaves before serving.

Lime Cucumber Raita

Yogurt based cooling sauces are usually associated with Middle Eastern or Indian cuisine but this one seems appropriate for this recipe. If possible, make it an hour ahead of time to allow the flavors to develop.

1 cup non-fat plain yogurt
½ cup Thai Kitchen Pure Coconut Milk (Regular or Lite)
1 cucumber, peeled, halved, seeded, and cut into ¼" dice
2 Tbs. lime juice
1 Tbs. palm sugar or white sugar
2 green onions, thinly sliced
¼ cup fresh cilantro, finely chopped
¼ cup mint*, finely chopped

In a bowl, combine yogurt, coconut milk, cucumber, lime juice, sugar, onions, cilantro and mint; mix well. Cover and refrigerate at least 1 hour. Serve with Red Curry Beef and Potato Fajitas, or use as a dip with your favorite chips or Thai meal.

* If fresh mint cannot be found, you can use your favorite basil.

Beef Noodle Soup

This hearty soup is almost like a meal in itself.

8 cups beef or chicken stock
1 cup carrots, sliced
1 Tbs. Thai Kitchen Premium Fish Sauce
1 tsp. soy sauce
1 stick cinnamon
2 whole star anise, pieces*
1 Tbs. garlic, minced
1 Tbs. ginger, minced
1 Tbs. rice vinegar
1 tsp. fresh chili pepper, minced
1 (7 oz.) package Thai Kitchen Thin Rice Noodles**
½ cup green onions, sliced
1 Tbs. lime juice
¾ lb. beef, thinly sliced
¼ cup roasted unsalted peanuts, crushed
½ cup fresh mint, cilantro and basil, julienned

In a heavy stockpot over medium-high heat combine stock, carrots, fish sauce, soy, cinnamon, star anise, garlic, ginger, vinegar, and chili. Bring to a boil, reduce heat to medium and simmer for 15 minutes to blend flavors. Add rice noodles, green onions and lime juice and simmer for 3 minutes. Add beef and cook until beef just colors (a minute or two at most). Adjust seasoning. Ladle into bowls and garnish with peanuts and mint, cilantro and basil. Makes 4 to 6 servings.

Note: The better quality beef that you use, the better this dish will taste. We recommend filet mignon.

* Star anise is optional in this recipe.
** For less starchy noodles that do not clump and stick together, soak noodles in hot tap water for 5 minutes. Rinse with cold water. Drain all water before adding to soup for cooking. See, Rice Noodle Preparation, page 201.

Hot & Sour Prawn Soup

Known as Tom Yum Kung in Thailand. This is the classic soup of Thailand. It can be made with chicken or tofu.

1 lb. prawns or large shrimp, shelled and deveined
6 cups fish stock, vegetable stock or 3 cups clam juice mixed with
       3 cups water
¼ cup rice vinegar
2 stalks fresh lemon grass*, thinly sliced
1 Tbs. fresh galangal (Thai ginger) or Chinese ginger, minced
4 kaffir lime leaves**
1 Tbs. Thai Kitchen Roasted Red Chili Paste
1 cup shiitake mushrooms, sliced
2 Tbs. Thai Kitchen Premium Fish Sauce
3 Tbs. fresh lime juice
2 Tbs. palm sugar or brown sugar
2 Tbs. fresh cilantro, chopped
Optional garnishes: 1 to 2 Thai chilies, sliced, and sprigs of fresh
       cilantro

Peel and devein prawns. In a large stockpot, combine stock and vinegar; bring to a boil. Reduce heat and bring to a simmer. Stir in lemon grass, galangal, kaffir lime leaves and roasted red chili paste; reduce heat and simmer for 5 minutes. In a bowl, combine fish sauce, lime juice and sugar; blend well to dissolve sugar. Add prawns, shiitake mushrooms and fish sauce mixture to stockpot and simmer until prawns are just cooked or turn orange-pink in color, about 1-2 minutes. Remove lemon grass and kaffir lime leaves before serving. Add chopped cilantro and chilies. Ladle into bowls. Garnish with sprigs of fresh cilantro. Makes 4 to 6 servings.

* Lemon grass is optional in this recipe. See, Lemon Grass, pages 194, 199.
** Kaffir lime leaves are optional in this recipe. See, Kaffir Lime Leaves, page 193.

Calamari Salad

Use very fresh squid. The key to this salad is quick poaching of the squid. You want to cook it fast so that it will be tender and crunchy.

8 oz. squid, cleaned
2 cups water
¼ cup red bell pepper, julienned
¼ cup sweet onion, finely chopped
¼ cup cucumber, diced
2 Tbs. green onions, thinly sliced
2 Tbs. Thai Kitchen Premium Fish Sauce
2 Tbs. fresh lime juice
1 Tbs. palm sugar or brown sugar
1-2 Thai chilies, seeded and minced
4 butter lettuce leaves, rinsed and dried
Optional garnish: fresh mint leaves

Cut squid into rings ¼-inch thick. In a small saucepan, bring water to a boil. Add squid and poach for 30 seconds or until just cooked. Drain and run under cold water. Place in a large salad bowl with bell pepper, onion, cucumber and green onions.

Dressing: In a small bowl, combine fish sauce, lime juice, sugar and chilies; stir until sugar is dissolved.

Drizzle dressing over squid mixture; toss lightly. Serve by spooning equal portions of salad into each lettuce cup. Garnish with mint leaves. Makes 4 servings.

Thai Barbecue Prawns

The secret of succulence is to be sure not to overcook the prawns. A standout party dish.

> 1 ½ lbs. prawns (25 to 30 count), or large shrimp
> ½ cup Thai Kitchen Thai Barbecue Sauce
> 2 tsp. kosher salt
> 2 tsp. ground white pepper
> 1 Tbs. olive oil
> peanut oil to coat pan
> *Optional garnish*: ½ cup finely chopped Thai basil or regular
>   basil

Peel, devein and butterfly prawns. Rinse thoroughly in cold water and place in bowl. Add Thai barbecue sauce, salt, pepper and olive oil and coat evenly. Refrigerate until ready to cook.

Heat a large non-stick frying pan over high heat and coat lightly with peanut oil. Test with a drop of water, if it sizzles in the pan, it is hot enough to begin cooking. Quickly place the prawns, butterflied side down, in pan. By the time you've filled the pan with prawns, the first ones should be done on the the first side. Use tongs to turn prawns on side. After you've turned them all to the side they should be ready to flip to the other side. Use tongs to turn to other side. The whole process will only take a few minutes, but does require constant attention. Prawns will be done when they are orange-pink in color and firm to the touch, about 1-2 minutes. Place prawns on a plate. If all the prawns didn't fit in the pan, wipe the pan with a paper towel to remove browned bits; lightly oil and repeat cooking steps.

Prawns may be served as is or tossed with ½ cup chopped Thai basil, if desired. Makes 8 to 10 servings.

Beef & Broccoli Stir-Fry with Green Curry

Once you taste this stir-fry, you'll understand how fast and easy it is to make authentic Thai food in an American kitchen.

1 lb. beef filet, sliced into thin strips
2 Tbs. olive oil
2 stalks broccoli, peeled and cut into ½" pieces
1 cup onion, diced
½ cup shallots, chopped
1 Tbs. garlic, minced
1 Tbs. ginger, minced
½ Tbs. lemon grass*, minced
1 cup Thai Kitchen Pure Coconut Milk (Regular or Lite)
1 cup beef stock or water
1 Tbs. Thai Kitchen Green Curry Paste
1 Tbs. Thai Kitchen Premium Fish Sauce
1 Tbs. lime juice
½ cup basil, julienned
Thai Kitchen Jasmine Rice

In a wok or sauté pan, brown beef quickly in olive oil over high heat for 1 minute. Remove and set aside. Pour all excess oil from pan, but do not clean. Add broccoli, onion, shallots, garlic, ginger and lemon grass and sauté for 4 minutes or until onion softens. Add coconut milk, stock, green curry paste, fish sauce and lime juice. Bring to a boil and reduce heat to medium. Simmer for 10 minutes. Return beef to the pan and add the basil and cook for 1 minute to heat through. Serve over cooked Thai Kitchen Jasmine Rice. Makes 4 servings.

* Lemon grass is optional in this recipe. See, Lemon Grass, pages 194, 199.

Grilled Red Curry Beef and Potato Fajitas with Lime Cucumber Raita

This Southeast/Southwest dish blends the cuisines of Thailand and Mexico (or at least the American Southwest). You might want to add some bell peppers to the grill.

3 Tbs. Thai Kitchen Red Curry Paste
3 Tbs. olive oil
2 lbs. skirt steak, trimmed
10 medium yellow Finn potatoes, or Russets, or yellow potatoes,
      peeled
3 large sweet onions, peeled and cut into ½" slices
12 flour tortillas
Lime Cucumber Raita (see page 145)

In a small bowl, combine red curry paste and olive oil; blend well. Evenly coat both sides of the steak with half of the curry mixture. Marinate for 30 minutes at room temperature.

Meanwhile, cut the potatoes in half lengthwise. Place in a stock pot with boiling water and boil for 8 minutes or until almost done, but still slightly firm; drain. Place the parboiled potatoes and onions in a large mixing bowl or zip lock bag and add the remaining red curry paste and coat well.

Prepare your grill. You'll want a hot fire for this one. Place the onion slices and potatoes, cut side down, on the edges of the grill and cook for 5 minutes on each side until there are grill marks on them. Place the steak in the center of the grill and cook for 3 minutes, turn and grill for 2 minutes more. Remove ingredients from the grill and allow them to stand 5 minutes to cool.

To serve, roughly chop the potatoes and onions. Slice the beef into thin slices across the grain and place on top of the onions and potatoes. Warm tortillas on your grill and allow your guests to roll their own using the Lime Cucumber Raita as a sauce.

Red Curry Glazed Roast Pork

The spiciness of the curry paste adds enough heat but if you really like it hot, add the chili sauce.

¼ cup Thai Kitchen Red Curry Paste
½ cup honey
2 Tbs. soy sauce
3 Tbs. olive oil
4 cloves garlic, mashed to a paste
2 Tbs. Thai Kitchen Spicy Thai Chili Sauce (optional)
4 to 5 lb. pork loin
3 cups onions, thinly sliced
Thai Kitchen Jasmine Rice

Combine red curry paste, honey, soy, olive oil, garlic and chili sauce; blend well. Coat pork loin on all sides with ½ of this mixture.

In a large baking pan, cover the bottom of pan with onions. Place pork on top of onions. Cook in a preheated 450°F oven for 10 minutes; reduce heat to 350°F and cook for an additional 1 to 1 ½ hours, turning and basting every 15 minutes with the remaining sauce. The pork is done when it reaches an internal temperature of 145°F, but if you aren't a fan of rosy pork, cook until it gets to 155°F. Allow pork and onions to cool 10 minutes.

Slice pork; drain and chop onions. Serve by placing a layer of onions over cooked Thai Kitchen Jasmine Rice and topping it with slices of pork. Serves 4 to 6.

Grilled Chicken Breast with Red Curry Rub

One of the biggest problems in grilling chicken breasts is timing. Brining is a method of of having perfectly juicy chicken breasts almost every time.

4 chicken breasts
½ cup kosher salt
½ cup sugar
1 qt. water
2 Tbs. Thai Kitchen Red Curry Paste
2 Tbs. peanut oil
3 Tbs. Thai Kitchen Thai Barbecue Sauce

Cut and separate chicken breasts into eight pieces. Dissolve salt and sugar in water in a zip lock bag. Add chicken breasts, seal bag and refrigerate for 1 ½ to 2 hours. Remove breasts from brine and dry thoroughly with paper towels. Rub each breast half on both sides with red curry paste.

Prepare grill with coals to one side. Brush grill lightly with oil. Grill breasts skin side down for 2 minutes over heat. Turn and grill for 2 minutes longer. Turn and move to other side of grill and cook on skin side again. Baste lightly with half of the Thai barbecue sauce and cook for 3 minutes. Turn, baste other side with barbecue sauce and continue cooking over indirect heat for 3 minutes. Remove from grill, let sit for 2 minutes. Slice each breast crosswise into smaller pieces. Makes 4 servings.

Prawns & Basil Green Curry

Do a little chopping earlier in the day, then stir-fry a delicious Thai meal in about 10 minutes.

2 Tbs. olive oil
1 cup sweet onion, thinly sliced
1 Tbs. ginger, minced
2 Tbs. garlic, minced
1 fresh chili, chopped
1 cup Thai Kitchen Pure Coconut Milk (Regular or Lite)
1 Tbs. Thai Kitchen Green Curry Paste
1 Tbs. Thai Kitchen Premium Fish Sauce
1 Tbs. lime juice
4 kaffir lime leaves*, minced
12 oz. large prawns, or12 oz. rock shrimp, shelled and deveined
¼ cup Thai basil, chopped
Thai Kitchen Jasmine Rice

In a sauté pan or wok, heat oil and sauté onion and ginger over high heat for 3 minutes. Add garlic, chili, coconut milk, green curry paste, fish sauce, lime juice and kaffir lime leaves and cook for 4 minutes; stirring to blend well. Add prawns and cook until prawns are just firm or orange-pink in color, about 1-2 minutes. Turn off heat. Add basil; stir lightly and serve over cooked Thai Kitchen Jasmine Rice. Serves 2.

* Kaffir lime leaves are optional in this recipe. See, Kaffir Lime Leaves, page 193.

Grilled Albacore with Red Curry

Grilling a whole fillet of fish can seem like a daunting proposition, but with a little practice, you'll have an impressive dish. Cooking the fish on one side is certainly easy enough, it's turning the fillet over that's the tricky part. Fish baskets make this a snap. The other main difficulty of grilling fish is that there isn't much room for error -- a piece can quickly go from perfectly cooked to dry. You've got to be paying constant attention. Ten minutes of cooking time per inch of thickness is a good standard. This recipe calls for an albacore loin, but any fillet of firm-fleshed fish such as halibut, bass or salmon will do.

> 4 to 5 lb. albacore loin
> 2 Tbs. Thai Kitchen Red Curry Paste
> ¼ cup Thai Kitchen Thai Barbecue Sauce
> 2 Tbs. peanut oil
> Thai Kitchen Jasmine Rice

Score skin side of the fish with ¼" deep cuts, about ½" apart. Combine red curry paste and barbecue sauce; mix well until blended. Coat both sides of fish with the red curry mixture.

Prepare grill or fish basket; lightly oil. Starting with the skin side down, grill fish for 5 minutes and then turn fish and grill 4 more minutes on the other side. Remove from grill and serve with cooked Thai Kitchen Jasmine Rice on the side. Serves 2 to 4.

Coconut Ginger Ice Cream

Most of the Thai recipes for coconut ice cream are more like sorbets. Our richer version makes a great complement to the baked pineapple. You will need an ice cream maker for this recipe.

1 (14 oz.) can Thai Kitchen Pure Coconut Milk (Regular or Lite)
½ cup whole milk
2 Tbs. ginger, minced
4 large eggs, yolks only
1/3 cup superfine sugar
½ cup fresh cream
2 Tbs. dark rum
Baked Pineapple (see page 157)

In a saucepan, combine coconut milk, milk and ginger. Heat until scalded. Remove from heat and allow to cool slightly.

In a bowl, combine egg yolks and sugar and beat with a whisk until fine yellow ribbons form (this will take a few minutes). Add ½ cup of the coconut milk mixture to eggs, whisking well to combine. Transfer this to a double boiler and add the remaining coconut milk mixture. Place double boiler over boiling water and continue stirring until mixture thickly coats the back of a wooden spoon. Remove from heat and allow to cool completely in refrigerator or in a bowl placed over an ice bath. When cool, strain through a fine sieve and add cream and rum; mix well.

Place in an ice cream maker and follow manufacturer's instructions until frozen.

Serve alone or with baked pineapple slices.

Baked Pineapple

The tropical taste of pineapple made more exotic!

1 pineapple, peeled, cored and cut into slices
¼ cup palm sugar or brown sugar
1 cup dark rum
Coconut Ginger Ice Cream (see page 156)
Optional garnish: candied ginger

Place pineapple slices in an oven-proof dish. Combine sugar and rum and pour over pineapple slices. Bake in a preheated 300°F oven, uncovered, for 1 hour or until liquid has completely evaporated and pineapple is soft. Place pineapple sections on plate. Declious alone or topped with coconut ginger ice cream. Garnish with chopped pieces of candied ginger. Makes 4 to 6 servings.

Coconut Custard Baked in a Pumpkin

Custard baked in a pumpkin is an old New England holiday dessert. It is also, with coconut milk, a popular dessert in Thailand. Thai recipes use kabocha squash instead of pumpkin. If you're serving chilled slices, caramel or chocolate sauce makes a nice, if untraditional, topping.

4 to 5 lb. pumpkin
2 cups Thai Kitchen Pure Coconut Milk (Regular or Lite)
1 cup whole milk
1 cup fresh cream
3 large whole eggs
2 large egg yolks
1/3 cup sugar
½ tsp. ground cardamom
½ tsp. ground allspice
¼ tsp. salt
¼ cup chopped candied ginger
Optional: ¼ cup dried cranberries

With a sharp knife, cut off top of pumpkin and set aside. With your hands or a spoon, clean out the inside of the pumpkin; removing all seeds and stringy bits.

In a saucepan, combine coconut milk, milk and cream and scald over medium heat. In a mixing bowl, beat eggs, egg yolks and sugar with electric mixer until fine yellow ribbons form. Stir in cardamom, allspice, and salt. Stirring continuously, add scalded coconut milk mixture, ginger and cranberries.

Pour into pumpkin shell. Add one inch of warm water to baking pan and place pumpkin in pan with top beside it. Bake for 1 ½ hours, checking custard periodically after an hour. Custard is done when knife comes out clean. This dish may be served hot from the oven, scooping custard out along with bits of pumpkin. It also makes an appealing cold presentation. Allow pumpkin to cool completely, then refrigerate. Remove just before serving and slice into wedges. Serves 8 to 10.

Coconut Lime Pie

Tart, sweet, tangy and exotic!

Crust:
2 cups ginger snaps, crumbled
2 Tbs. flour
4 Tbs. unsalted butter, chilled

Filling:
4 egg yolks
1 (14 oz.) can Thai Kitchen Pure Coconut Milk (Regular or Lite)
2/3 cup sweetened condensed milk
2 envelopes unflavored gelatin
½ cup water
2/3 cup fresh lime juice

Topping:
4 egg whites
¼ cup sugar

Combine ginger snaps, flour and butter in a food processor and process until completely blended. Place crumb mixture in a 9" pie pan and press firmly into pan to form crust. Bake for 7 minutes in a 350°F preheated oven. Remove and allow to cool completely.

With a whisk, beat egg yolks until smooth. Combine coconut milk, condensed milk and egg yolks in a saucepan. Bring to a simmer, stirring constantly. Reduce heat, continue stirring, and simmer 10 minutes or until mixture thickens and coats side of spoon and pan. Remove from heat. In a microwave safe bowl, combine gelatin and water; soften in the microwave on high temperature for one minute or until gelatin is completely dissolved. Stir in lime juice. Add this gelatin mixture to the saucepan with milk and eggs mixture; mix well. Allow to cool completely. Pour filling into cooled, prebaked pie crust.

Whip the egg whites until soft peaks form. Add sugar and continue beating, until stiff but not dry. Cover the pie filling with the beaten egg whites.

Place pie in pre-heated 350°F oven for 10 minutes or until meringue topping is lightly browned. Makes one 9" pie.

Fried Yams

I've always loved fried yams at Thai restaurants. This is my version of the dish. A great side dish for a main course.

2 lbs. yams
½ cup all-purpose flour
½ cup masa (corn flour)
½ tsp. baking soda
¾ tsp. allspice
¾ tsp. ground black pepper
1/8 tsp. salt
2 eggs
1 (14 oz.) can Thai Kitchen Pure Coconut Milk (Regular or Lite)

Peel yams and cut into ½" slices. In a bowl, combine flour, masa, baking soda, allspice, pepper, and salt; mix well. Stir in eggs and coconut milk; blend well. The batter should be thick enough to coat the yam slices. Adjust thickness with more coconut milk or flour as necessary. In a wok or heavy skillet heat oil to 325°F over high heat. Dip yam slices into batter and fry until golden brown all over. Drain on absorbent paper towels. Serves 2 to 3.

Glossary

The Essence of Thai Cuisine
-- In Balance With Nature.

In some of our ingredient descriptions, we will provide you with the Asian medicinal theories behind commonly used Thai Kitchen ingredients. In our products, herbs are used in many forms – fresh, dried or ground. When preparing our products, we strive for a balance of color, texture and flavor. We carefully use herbs for their flavor contributions as well as to reestablish the balance between *Yin & Yang* – a cosmic equilibrium of the harmony of all things. Although *Yin & Yang* is known as a Chinese philosophy, with Thailand's close proximity and large Chinese population, these principles have been adopted into Thai cooking. It is the idea of two opposing forces in balance. *Yin* represents the cooler, moist and weaker forces, while *Yang* is the warm, dry and stronger forces. Thai cooks follow this philosophy by selecting a combination of foods that balance these forces. Finished cooked dishes are evaluated both on the delicious results and on how they affect the body. *"Cold"* or *Yin* foods sooth and cleanse the body. Chili peppers, ginger, galangal and lemon grass are known as *"hot"* sensuous *Yang* foods as they increase the pulse rate and trigger perspiration. It is thought that when the *Yin & Yang* forces are not in equilibrium, illness occurs. These theories have been handed down from generation to generation. Many believe these theories to be fact while some feel that they are only myth. We encourage you to be the judge.

Anise, Star *(poy kak bua)*: The tan-colored pods with eight points, like stars, come from trees in the Magnolia family. Used in Thailand primarily in dishes of Chinese origin, star anise is unrelated to anise, but imparts a similar licorice flavor to dishes. Commonly found in Five-Spice Powder, it is more often added whole to curries and soups.

Bamboo Shoots *(nor mai)*: The young shoots of the bamboo plant. Available in many different sizes and forms. The most common is canned, however you can usually find them fresh soaking in some water at an Asian supermarket. They are pale yellow in color and usually crispy and crunchy to the taste with a mild flavor. They are used for color, texture, and flavor in many Thai dishes. We recommend soaking them in cold water with some salt for at least 20 minutes to lessen any canned or stale taste. They will keep in the refrigerator for up to two weeks in water. The water should be changed daily.

Banana Leaves *(bai tong)*: In Thai cooking, banana leaves are used to wrap food for steaming, baking or grilling; and made into cups to hold custards and salads. In Mexican cuisine they are sometimes used instead of cornhusks to wrap tamales. They are occasionally available fresh, but can be most commonly found frozen in Asian or Mexican markets. Defrost before using and wash well in hot water. Leftover leaves may be rewrapped and re-frozen.

Basil *(bai gra pao)*: The Thai people cherish basil almost as much as the Genovese. Fresh basil is the best for full, fresh flavors. Leaves are picked off the stem and added directly into soups, stir-fries and other dishes. Thais use basil the same way other cultures use basil – as a fresh herb. However, Thais also enjoy it as a vegetable, a condiment, and a garnish for many dishes. Three varieties are used in Thai cooking: Thai Basil, Sweet Basil, and Lemon Basil *(see following detailed descriptions)*.

Basil, Dried *(gra pao haeng)*: Makes a nice filling for potpourri satchels, but is useless to cook with.

Basil, Thai *(bai grapao) / Thai Holy Basil*: The most common in Thai cooking. This is the closest basil to the European herb found in tomato-based recipes and pesto. It has small pointed, serrated bright green leaves, with distinct reddish-purplish stalks and honeycomb shaped buds. It is the most mint-like in flavor.

Basil, Thai Lemon *(bai mangluk)*: Has small, hairy, paler-green leaves and a distinct tangy, citrus flavor. It releases a lemon scent and a peppery taste when chewed. Very similar to Italian Dwarf Basil, it is used as a vegetable and for flavoring. Thais also use Lemon Basil as a condiment or garnish for many dishes.

Basil, Thai Sweet *(bai horapa)*: Used as a vegetable and for flavoring. When fresh and cooked it imparts a natural, slightly strong, sweet anise *(licorice)* flavor and fragrance. Thai sweet basil is commonly found chopped or ground in curries and pastes.

Basil, Seeds *(ma led graprao)*: Are popular in desserts, becoming gelatinous when soaked in water and cooked. The best source for basil is growing your own. It thrives in an indoor planter with lots of sun.

Bean Curd: *(see, Tofu)*.

Bean Curd, Fermented/Pickled Soy *(too hu yee)*: A pickled tofu that has a soft, almost custard-like smooth texture with a strong salty taste and a pungent wine aroma. There are many different varieties. The most common types are white and yellow. Usually sold in cakes or in small cubes in jars. The white variety is usually pickled with sesame oil, rice wine and chili. The red variety is made using red rice wine, chili, and annato seeds. Its distinct, pungent flavor is commonly used in place of salt or fish sauce to flavor a stir-fry, soup or steamed entrée. Used commonly as a flavoring for rice porridge (congee).

Bean Sprouts *(tua ngawk)*: Are typically mung bean sprouts but soybean sprouts are sometimes available. Sprouts have bright silver white bodies with yellow or green heads and small thin hair-like tails. Often used in stir-fry dishes, soups and salads. When buying bean sprouts, choose dry, firm, white spouts. Best when used the same day of purchase but will keep in a refrigerator (in an open bag so that moisture can escape) for a few days. Unsprouted mung beans are small round green beans that are easy to grow. The seeds are usually available in Chinese grocery stores or in health food stores. Soak a quarter of a cup of mung beans in water overnight. Spread a thin layer of the soaked beans on a wet newspaper or cheesecloth on a cookie sheet. Place them in a warm dark area (inside an off oven is ideal). They will sprout and be ready to eat in about five days when the roots are about two inches long.

Bean Thread Noodles *(woon sen) / Clear Noodles, Glass Noodles, Sai Fun, Mung Bean Vermicelli, Jelly Noodles, Cellophane Noodles:* A thin, angel hair-width noodle made from mung bean starch, derived from fresh bean sprouts. These noodles are commonly found in soup-noodle dishes and cold salads. In the dry stage, they are white in appearance and look like a bunch of tangled string but should not be confused with rice vermicelli. Although they look similar when dried and in the package, bean thread noodles become transparent and jelly-like when cooked. Their delicate flavor is perfect for soups. These noodles absorb a lot of soup, therefore it is recommended to use a lot of broth and small amounts of noodles, as you will see your soup disappear in front of your eyes. They are often fried and used as a garnish for Asian salads. For frying, there is no need to soak the noodles. You fry them in a dry stage. Be prepared to fish them out of the hot oil immediately as they will puff up like popcorn as soon as they hit the oil. When frying they are ready in a manner of seconds. To prepare noodles for stir-frying or soups, soak them in warm water for a few minutes until they are soft, but firm and not mushy. Drain with cold water before cooking. Wheat-free, gluten-free, fat-free, cholesterol-free, egg-free, this is a delicious noodle with versatile uses and many different names.

Bergamot: *(see, Kaffir Lime).*

Bird's-Eye Chili: *(see, Chilies).*

Bok Choy *(phug glad goung toong):* A white stemmed, loose leafed vegetable in the cabbage family. The stems are usually seven to nine inches tall with a mild, tangy, pepper taste. The trunks are crunchy and the leaves are soft. There is also baby bok choy: young bok choy picked early. Another variety, the Shanghai, has jade green, spoon shaped trunks and curved leaves. Both the baby and the Shanghai variety are sweeter and less fibrous than the regular and are delicious lightly stir-fried to release their natural sweetness. Trim the stem ends and slice the trunks diagonally. The baby bok choy can usually be cooked whole, or cut in quarters or halves. When buying bok choy, look for firm trunks with a bright green color. Store in the refrigerator up to a week.

Broccoli, Chinese *(ka na)*: A dark green vegetable with strong, thin, long round trunks, soft, deep green delicate leaves, and sometimes tiny white flowers. It does not look like or taste like the common broccoli. It has a slightly sweet and bitter taste. Delicious stir-fried, steamed, or boiled but never eaten raw. Unlike regular broccoli, the stems are usually tender and do not need to be peeled. However, more mature or larger stalks should be peeled before cooking. It is always smart to separate the leaves and trunks. The trunks require more cooking time, then add the leaves near the end, so that they cook evenly. When buying Chinese broccoli, choose brightly colored ones with slender thin trunks.

Calrose Rice *(kao jao)*: A short grain rice.

Cardamom *(luk kra wan)*: A native of India and Sri Lanka, it also grows in Thailand near the Cambodia border. The green, white or black seedpods must be cracked open to extract the cool, strong scented small black seeds, which are then ground. The pods and seeds are popular in different types of sweet or savory Thai dishes, especially curries. They are often mixed with ginger and boiled, as a health drink. In addition to its culinary role, cardamom has a sexy history as a perfume and an aphrodisiac. Medically, it has been used as a laxative and to relieve indigestion. Europeans have called it Siamese cardamom since the 17th Century. It was one of the first spices exported to England, China and Japan. By weight, cardamom is one of the most expensive spices, exceeded only by vanilla and saffron. As it quickly loses much of its flavor when ground, it's best to buy whole pods and crack them open and grind the seeds yourself. This plant needs a humid climate to grow.

Cassava Plant: *(see, Tapioca Pearls)*.

Cellophane Noodles: *(see, Bean Thread Noodles)*.

Chilies *(phrik)*: A general rule is: the smaller the chili, the hotter it is and the larger chili is milder. Chilies are rich in vitamin C and are thought to aid in digestion. The hottest parts of the chili are the seeds. Mature chilies are always a darker color than young ones. It is the oil substance called capsaicin, which is concentrated in the seeds and inside the membranes, that make chilies hot. If you accidentally eat chilies and your mouth burns, do not drink water – rice, beer or milk drinks will help relieve the burn. Scientists believe that chilies are native to Central America and that they were brought to Thailand and the Far East by the Portuguese in the 16th Century. This means that Thai food has been "hot" for only the last 400 years. Many Thais are reluctant to believe this, arguing that chilies may have come from across the Pacific or that they originated in Central Asia and were taken by Mongoloid people to the New World. They also argue that chilies have been used for centuries as a medicine as well as a condiment, to lower blood pressure and cholesterol. According to food scientist Harold McGee, more people now consume chili peppers in larger quantities than any other spice in the world. This is certainly true in Thailand. Even in America, the growing demand (you might even call it a burning desire) for fiery food has made a wide variety of the members of the Capsicum family available fresh. The most common hot chili in Thailand is a small slender chili called *prik kii noo* or "bird's eye chili," rated the second hottest chili, coming in just under the habañero. The "bird's eye chili" is also known as the "mouse-dropping chili," which has to be the all-time least-appetizing food name. The equivalent chili we suggest is the serrano. It is possible to reduce the heat of a chili by scraping the seeds. Some cookbooks recommend wearing rubber gloves when working with chilies. Be sure to wash thoroughly your cutting board, knives and hands afterwards. Bell peppers are not traditionally Thai, but we use them in this book to please the non-Thai palate. In recent years, a chili imported from Mexico called *prik khee noo kaset*, which has longer pods than *prik kii noo*, is commonly used in Thai cooking.

Chilies, Dried *(phrik haeng)*: An essential component in the preparation of some Thai curries and sauces. The heat depends on what kind it is, and in most cases you should be able to substitute a dried American or Mexican chili. The seeds of these chilies are very hot, much hotter than the pods. Dried chilies are also hotter than fresh ones. Dried chilies are widely available in Mexican markets and health food stores.

Chinese Ginger: *(see, Ginger)*.

Chinese Long Beans: *(see, Long Beans)*.

Chinese Parsley: *(see, Cilantro)*.

Cilantro *(pak chi) / Coriander, Chinese Parsley, Mexican Parsley*: This savory herb with flat green leaves and a refreshingly herbaceous taste is one of the staples of Thai cuisine. Known around the world as an herb and for flavoring, it has been used for thousands of years in Asia. It is delightfully aromatic with a distinct spiced grass/herb taste. This parsley should not be confused with Italian parsley, which has curly leaves. This is much more flavorful and fragrant. Essentially, three parts of cilantro are used in Thai cooking: leaves, roots and seeds. Each has a unique flavor and character. The fresh leaves are plucked off the stem and used as a garnish or mixed into the food. Thai cooks crush the roots and stems into pastes and chili sauces. The Thais seem to be the only people to use the roots in their cuisine. The seeds *(mellet pak chee)* bear no taste resemblance in flavor to the plant. The seeds are usually found in curries and soups. Cilantro is thought to have originated in the Mediterranean about 3,000 years ago. It is a relative of the carrot. It also features small white or pink flowers. Cilantro is available all year round. If you would like to grow cilantro from seeds, the best time is around March or April. Plant the seeds loosely, cover lightly with soil, expose to light, keep humid and warm until they sprout. When buying cilantro, choose a bunch with fresh leaves and stems. To store, place it into a bowl of water and cover the top loosely with plastic wrap. It will keep in the refrigerator up to two weeks. Cilantro is optional in many recipes. If you cannot find it in your market, or if you do not like the taste, you might substitute flat leaf parsley or even basil.

Cinnamon *(op choey):* True cinnamon is the sweetly aromatic dried tan-colored inner bark of an evergreen native to Sri Lanka. Much of what is sold as cinnamon in the Western countries is more strongly scented and darker-colored. In Thailand, the Batavia variety is the most common. It often adds a pleasant flavor and aroma to beef and chicken dishes. Medically, it has been used as an anti-acid and is thought to be able to reduce any overproduction of a nursing mother's milk.

Claypot Rice Noodles: *(see, Rice Noodles).*

Clear Noodles: *(see, Bean Thread Noodles).*

Cloves *(kan phlu):* Made from the dried flower buds of an evergreen tree native to Molucca (one of the appropriately called Spice Islands), cloves impart a sharply heady flavor that is often used to balance the rich flavor of meats. A member of the myrtle family, they can be used whole or in powder form. They are delicious with tomatoes, salty vegetables and ham. In Thailand, cloves are chewed like a candy and as a relief for toothaches. Medically, Thais believe that cloves kill bacteria and control spasms, and that they aid in digestion. This spice is expensive because crops often fail. A Thai favorite, Masuman curry paste features the distinctive bite of cloves.

Coconut Milk *(nam kathee):* Known as the milk of Asia, it is one of the essential foundations of Thai cooking. Coconut milk has a variety of uses: in cooking, sauces, drinks, curries and desserts. It is made in a method similar to that of olive oil. Mature brown coconuts are cracked open. The meat is scraped from the shells and the thin brown skin is removed from the meat. The meat is soaked in water then blended. The meat/water is squeezed and strained to extract as much liquid as possible. The liquid that rises to the top (separating from the water) is coconut milk. The first pressing of the meat is pure coconut milk *(hua ga-ti or nam katee* "head of the coconut milk"). The milk extracted from the first pressing has the highest fat content (between 22%-24%). Thai Kitchen Pure Coconut Milk is made from the first pressing and may be used in recipes calling for either coconut milk or coconut cream. This process is repeated again using previously squeezed coconut meat to yield a lighter coconut milk *(hahng-ti)* "tail of the coconut milk." The second pressing of the meat produces a fat content of 12%-14%. Thai Kitchen Pure Coconut Milk Lite has about half the fat and calories of our regular milk. It is not uncommon for coconut milk to separate. Some recipes call for coconut cream. For coconut cream, use Thai Kitchen Pure Coconut Milk or, for a richer flavor, spoon off the top layer of an unshaken/unstirred can of coconut milk. Coconut milk can be refrigerated for a few days or frozen. It should be thoroughly stirred before use. Coconuts (Maprao) are ubiquitous in Thailand.

Coconut Milk, Lite: *(see, Coconut Milk)*.

Coconut Sugar *(nam tan peep) / Palm Sugar*: Coconut Sugar and Palm Sugar (there are subtle differences between them, but they are sold interchangeably) are the most common sugars found in Thai cooking. These basic sugar sweeteners have a caramel, toffee-like flavor and aroma. They are produced from the sap of the coconut or sugar palms much like maple sugar is harvested in this country. Sold in compressed cakes that keep well in a tightly sealed jar, they are widely available in Asian markets. To make palm sugar, sap is collected from various palm trees (most common is the Palmyra Palm), boiled down to a thick syrup, which is poured into bamboo pipe molds. Once dried, it forms into deep brown crumbly round cylinders. These are then crumbled or granulated to a more usable form. Palm sugar adds a smooth, very full-bodied, rich sweet flavor. Thais use palm sugar to balance strong hot flavors such as curries. It complements the spicy, salty and sour tastes of Thai cuisine. Brown sugar can be substituted, although it will not be as rich or intense.

Coconuts, Young *(ma prao oon)*: Are a light green color and contain a clear coconut juice that is clean and refreshing to drink. It is very different than the juice from mature brown coconuts. The flesh of young coconuts is transparent and soft and is often used in desserts, the juice may be sold as a refreshing drink. In Thailand you will see people walking around with young green coconuts in hand, drinking the juice from a straw.

Coriander: *(see, Cilantro).*

Cumin *(yaa-raa)*: Native to the Middle East, (Egypt), it is used extensively in Thai cuisine (as well as the cuisines of Central and South America, Scandinavia, and North Africa). This small rigid, light brown seed is similar to caraway and fennel, and needs to be heated or cooked to release its full flavor. Mainly used for making Thai curries.

Curry Paste *(nam prik)*: Thais traditionally have made curry pastes fresh daily at home from scratch for their meal preparation. Sitting with a large stone mortar and pestle, the preparer makes small batches, grinding by hand the fresh chilies, garlic, kaffir lime leaves, onion and aromatic spices into a fresh paste. Today, however, modern work schedules have many Thais buying curry pastes from the vendors on the streets or in the market halls. At Thai Kitchen, we use the traditional methods for making our curry pastes so you know you're buying an authentic paste. *(Also see, Curry Paste, page 199.)*

Curry Paste, Green *(gaeng keow wan)*: Traditionally, green curry paste is the hottest of the curries. It is made from a combination of hot green peppers, garlic, kaffir lime leaf and galangal. *(Also see, Curry Paste, Thai Kitchen Green, page 193 and Curry Paste, page 199.)*

Curry Paste, Masuman *(gaeng musuman)*: A roasted red Thai curry paste made with cardamom, lemon grass, cinnamon, cloves, chilies and other spices with a distinct spicy flavor. Red Curry Paste with a little cardamom and sugar can be substituted. *(Also see, Curry Paste, page 199.)*

Curry Paste, Panang *(gaeng panang)*: A Thai curry paste made with red chilies, onion, garlic, galangal, lemon grass and kaffir lime. A wonderfully complex and interesting flavor. *(Also see, Curry Paste, page 199.)*

Curry Paste, Red Curry *(gang pa nang)*: High on the heat scale and very similar to green curry paste, using red peppers instead of green. Green curry paste is generally hotter. *(Also see, Curry Paste, Thai Kitchen Red, page 193, and Curry Paste, page 199).*

Curry Paste, Yellow *(gaeng leung)*: A milder paste made from yellow wax peppers. In addition to the other Thai herbs used, turmeric is added to enhance the deep yellow color. This curry paste most resembles Indian curry. Many of the influences from their neighbors are apparent in this Thai staple. *(Also see, Curry Paste, page 199.)*

Eggplant, Thai *(ma khua)*: Thai eggplants come in many different varieties and shapes. The small round ones *(ma khua khun)*, are the most commonly used variety and are about the size of ping-pong balls and are pale green, yellow or white in color. These are often eaten raw with a chili sauce. In curries, they have little taste but a very interesting texture; they act as a thickening agent (much like okra) as well as impart a delicate flavor. The pea-like, berry size eggplants *(ma khua puang)* have a slightly bitter taste and are added uncooked to chili sauces, pickled for curry paste, or used as a garnish for green curries. The long ones *(ma khua yao)*, sometimes called Japanese eggplant, are usually purple but may be pale green or white; these are usually cooked or put into a stir-fry. The hairy, small orange type *(ma uk)*, must have the hairs scraped off before being crushed as an ingredient in chili sauces or curry pastes. Thai eggplants are relatively seedless and do not need to be salted, soaked or peeled. Cut them into lengthwise or fan cut slices to grill, and for stir-frying or braising. Choose firm, unbruised, smooth and unblemished eggplant. Best used the day of purchase, but can be refrigerated for several days.

Eggroll Wrapper *(pan hoa poi pieh)*: Thin sheets of dough that are made from wheat flour, eggs, and water. They come in two shapes; round or square. Both shapes are popular. When fried, egg roll wrappers will have a bumpy, crispy and bubbly surface. The wrapper will turn semi-hard. Thicker than spring roll wrappers. *(Also see, Spring Roll Wrappers and Rice Paper Wrappers.)*

Fish Sauce *(nam pla)*: The main flavoring ingredient in Thai cuisine, it is commonly referred to as the soy sauce of Southeast Asia. Fish sauce is a thin, amber-tinted, clear liquid with a salty taste extracted from fermented salted fish (most commonly anchovies). Different combinations of fish (including mackerel, squid, and shrimp) and their quality will affect the taste. The anchovies are salted and placed in wooden casks to age from six weeks to six months. The richly flavored first liquid siphoned from the fermented anchovies is the most prized and is usually reserved for dipping sauces or for special occasions. The anchovies from the first fermentation are usually then used again. Water and salt are added a second time, and the pressed anchovies are fermented again. This lesser quality liquid is used for everyday eating and cooking. Thai Kitchen Premium Fish Sauce is premium quality. That means it is the liquid from the first fermentation of carefully selected premium quality salted anchovies, aged up to 18 months for an extra-rich, smooth, well-balanced, extra-virgin flavor. Thai Kitchen Premium Fish Sauce has no added water and no added sugar. Use it in place of salt or soy sauce to season almost any savory dish or stir-fry. Fish sauce has a distinct pungent aroma. The fragrant aroma will mellow with cooking or when added to food. Although now known as a seasoning of Southeast Asia, the origins of fish sauce trace back to the first millennium B.C. in China. Its popularity declined in China about two thousand years ago due to the popularity of fermented bean and vegetable sauces, precursors to the common soy sauce. Fish sauce is also found in Japanese and Korean dishes. Even the Romans had a taste for it, using a thick, fermented fish sauce called liquamen or garum. Sauces from different Southeast Asian countries yield different flavor characteristics. Vietnamese fish sauce tends to be sweet in flavor. Sugar is usually added to the fermentation process. Philippine fish sauce is heavier to flavor the country's bold, salty and sour flavors. For first time users, the taste and smell will require some time to accept and to get used to. However, once you discover the distinct and complex delicious flavor, you will never want to use salt or soy sauce again. Without this flavor, Thai dishes won't taste Thai. With the growing popularity of the cuisines of these countries, fish sauce is widely available in Asian markets, supermarkets and health food stores. Fish sauce should be refrigerated after opening. Because salt is used in the fermentation process, salt crystals appearing like glass or plastic fragments may naturally form in the bottle. These crystals will dissolve with cooking. (Also see, Fish Sauce, page 193.)

Galangal (khaa) / Siamese Ginger: A root, similar to ginger, that has a thin opaque yellow skin and dark growth rings on its skin with fibrous, woody shoots that grow from the core. The roots are larger and whiter. This rhizome has a distinctively lemon-y pungency and is more commonly available in this country in a dried form. It looks very similar to young ginger. Unlike ginger that is often eaten, the fibrous galangal slices should be removed from the food before serving. Galangal has a distinct medicinal, ginger taste. It is used in soups to chase the germs of a common cold out of your system. Spice traders brought it to Medieval Europe where it was highly prized, giving its name to the Western cooking term Galantine. It has a history as an aphrodisiac or a digestive stimulant. Mixed with lime juice, Thais use it as a cure for stomach aches. It is a basic ingredient in Thai curry pastes, and slices are usually added to fish or soup stocks. The flowers are edible. Thais batter and deep fry the flowers and serve them with a hot chili sauce. *(Also see, Galangal, page 193.)*

Garlic *(kra thiam)*: Almost as ubiquitous as fish sauce in Thai cuisine. White garlic is the most commonly found variety, but recently organic farmers have been reintroducing heirloom varieties. Thais are fond of fried garlic. Garlic is thinly sliced and fried into chips. To make fried garlic, peel and slice garlic, fry in hot oil until golden brown. This garlic is used as a garnish or a topping for any dish. Sprinkle it on top of soups or stir-fries. The oil in which the garlic is fried is saved and used in cooking to give food more flavor.

Ginger *(gaeng) / Chinese Ginger*: A mildly spiced root, which yields a spicy, aromatic taste. Its unique flavor is another constant in Thai cooking. Ginger is a knobby, brown thick root with a fibrous yellow interior. Young ginger will have a smooth, shiny, golden-yellow appearance with a delicate flavor and is not as stringy as mature ginger. Ginger is known to relieve coughing, nausea and dizziness. It is also thought to aid in digestion. It has a very distinct medicinal flavor. It is used in soups to chase the germs of a common cold out of your system. Widely available in supermarkets, look for firm shiny roots that are not dry or wrinkled. Young ginger is not as widely available but grab it if you come across it. Slice thinly with a mandolin or vegetable peeler, marinate in two cups of rice wine vinegar and a tablespoon of sugar, and you've got pickled ginger. Young ginger is also made into a candied form that is usually sold packed in syrup.

Ginger, Preserved *(gaeng dong)*: Young ginger is cured in salt and water, then soaked in a sugar and vinegar solution for a tangy-sweet, pungent ginger taste that is smoother and sweeter than fresh ginger. Opened jars of pickled ginger should be refrigerated. Thais use preserved ginger in all types of dishes and sauces.

Glass Noodles: *(see, Bean Thread Noodles).*

Glutinous Rice: *(see, Sticky Rice).*

Holy Basil: *(see Basil, Thai).*

Japanese Eggplant: *(see Eggplant, Thai).*

Jasmine Flowers *(mali)*: Unopened flowers buds, picked in the evening before they open, are used to scent drinking water, teas and desserts.

Jasmine Rice *(khao chao)*: This non-glutinous, long-grained rice with its subtle floral aroma is the main staple of the Thai diet. Distinctively nutty and aromatic, with a hint of natural jasmine flavor, it is a delightful complement to Asian and Western dishes. Most all the jasmine rice grown in the world is from Thailand. The tremendous demand from world markets has made this one of Thailand's most prized staples and main export items. Harvested just once a year from Thailand's fertile central plains, you'll agree jasmine rice could be the most delicious rice you will ever eat. *(Also see, Rice/Preparing and Cooking, page 199.)*

Jelly Noodles: *(see, Bean Thread Noodles).*

Kaffir Lime *(ma grut) / Thai Lime, Bergamot*: In Thailand almost every part of this plant is used in cooking. It is quite different from the lime that we are used to seeing here in the USA. The fruit has dark, wrinkled, bumpy skin, which is used in the preparation of

Thai curries. The leaves are highly prized for the unique citrus-floral note that they impart to soups and curries. The flavor is unique with its citrus-floral, lemon, geranium taste and scent. The peel and leaves can be found in Asian markets in dried form; if unavailable, the best alternative is lime zest. Most of the limes that appear in American markets are the Persian limes. When the recipes in this book call for lime juice, the juice of either lime is fine. Kaffir lime is difficult to find in the continental United States. It has been successfully grown on the Hawaiian Islands and has been experimentally grown in California for over 65 years. Kaffir lime is a very slow growing plant; it does not bear fruit until it is eight to ten years old. The juice is usually squeezed over dishes to give it a tangy flavor, the peel and leaves are ground and used in curries or in soups to give them a lime zest. Historically, the Thais used the juice in ointments and shampoos, and the peel in tonic medications. It was thought that the distinct essence drove away evil spirits. *(Also see, Kaffir Lime Leaves, page 193.)*

Lemon Grass *(ta krai):* A lemony and fragrant herb commonly used in teas, soups and pastes. The flavor of lemon grass is one of the essential tastes of Thai cuisine. Lemon grass comes in tall thick stalks with tough outer leaves that sheath a tender inner core. This woody yellow green stalk resembles tall (12"-24") fibrous grass blades. However, to relax or induce a sweat to cure a cold, Thais will chew on the ends of lemon grass stalks. In Thailand, lemon grass soup is used in place of chicken soup as a home cold remedy. Lemon grass is commercially grown in India, Australia, Africa, South America and the United States (Florida and recently California). It is possible to grow lemon grass in other parts of the United States. Check with your local nursery or plant shop. *(Also see, Lemon Grass, pages, 194, 199.)*

Long Beans *(thua fak yao) / Chinese Long Beans:* Botanically closer to the black-eyed pea than green beans, the long bean grows to a length of two to three feet. Chopped into pieces, it can be stir-fried, deep-fried or included in a stew or curry. In Thailand it is often minced and used as an ingredient in dressings and curries.

Mace *(dawk chand):* The orange outer covering of nutmeg which is the fruit of the evergreen tree native to Indonesia. Used in Thailand for making Musuman curry. *(see, Nutmeg).*

Mexican Parsley: *(see, Cilantro).*

Mint *(bai sa ra nae)*: Though closely related to the ubiquitous basil, mint is not nearly as widely used. Its introduction is said to be a result of the spread of Vietnamese cuisine. Thais use mint as a garnish, a vegetable and a flavoring agent to add that last little grace note of bracing coolness. Spearmint is the most commonly used variety in Thailand. The mint is similar to the mint grown in England.

Mushrooms, Black: *(see, Mushrooms, Shiitake).*

Mushrooms, Shiitake *(het hom)* / *Chinese Black Mushrooms:* Japanese shiitake and Chinese black mushrooms are similar varieties, used dried. The Japanese mushrooms have a slightly salty, musky, meaty flavor. Both varieties need to be soaked in hot or cold water for at least half and hour to hydrate and soften before using. The longer they soak, the softer they become. After soaking, trim off the knobby, woody stem ends before using. These mushrooms are delicious when stir-fried with vegetables. They are thought to stimulate the immune system, promote blood circulation, and lower cholesterol. Chinese black mushrooms are a cousin of the Japanese shiitake mushroom. They look similar in appearance, however, they have light tan creases on their cap. The Chinese black mushroom has a wild mushroom flavor slightly different that of the shiitake. These mushrooms are slightly less expensive than shiitake.

Mushrooms, Straw *(hed fang)*: Small delicate brown mushrooms with a sweet and meaty taste. They come in two forms. One form resembles small brown eggs. The cap of the mushroom encases the whole body and the stem. The peeled variety has a dark brown, domed-shaped cap and a short, thick stem. These mushrooms grow in rice straw (which gives them their name), and are available all year. Straw mushrooms are also commonly sold in cans. To use them, drain the can liquid and rinse the mushrooms with cold water. You might want to soak the mushrooms in cold water and salt for about 20 minutes to remove the canned taste.

Nutmeg *(luk chand)*: It is the seed of an elegant low growing tree that is native to the Moluccas Islands (Spice Islands) and all over Indonesia. The beige colored oval nut is protected by an orange-red, fibrous, strong, hard, web-like outer husk that is removed and processed to make mace. The nuts are slowly dried above a smoking fire for six weeks. This adds to their fragrant and sweet qualities. Popular in Europe since the 16th century. In Asia, nutmeg is a important ingredient for making curries, sauces and spice mixtures. It is often used in desserts, sweetmeats and to make Musuman curry paste *(see, Mace)*.

Onions *(hua hom)*: The onion family includes garlic, leeks, shallots, scallions and chives as well as a diverse selection of red, white, yellow and sweet onions.

Oyster Flavored Sauce, Chinese *(nam mun hoi)*: A thick brown sauce that is commonly used as a base sauce in Chinese food. Made from fermented oyster extracts and spices, it has a distinct and pleasant smoky-sweet flavor. Used in Chinese cuisine since 1888. Does not taste like oysters at all. The meaty, gravy taste gives food a distinct Chinese flavor.

Palm Sugar: *(see, Coconut Sugar)*.

Pho Noodles: *(see, Rice Noodles)*.

Prawns, Tiger *(kung kula dam)*: They have distinctive black and white stripes and are the largest among Asian prawns. These giant prawns can grow over twelve inches long. Large shrimp can be substituted. *(see, Shrimp)*.

Prik Kii Noo: *(see, Chili)*.

Rice Noodles, Dried *(kui teow)*: Made from rice flour and water, steamed until cooked, and then dried. Flat and slightly translucent, they are available in several widths. Thai Kitchen produces three varieties. All are dry and must be soaked or boiled before using. Thai Kitchen Thin Rice Noodles [also known as Rice Vermicelli *(sen mee)*, Claypot Noodles, Soup Noodles] are thin vermicelli noodles that are delicious served cold with a spicy topping, stir-fried, or a pleasing addition to soups. Thai Kitchen Stir-Fry Rice Noodles (also known as Rice Stick, Pho Rice Noodles) are linguini-width, perfect for Pad Thai and other stir-fried dishes. The Wide-Style Rice Noodles (also known as Rice Stick, Pho Rice Noodles) are rice noodles that are a wide fettuccini width, almost a ½ inch wide, and the preferred noodle for Lad Nah, Thai Noodles in Gravy. Rice noodles can be used in place of rice for curries and stews. Rice noodles, when dried and packaged, resemble tangled rolls of string. All varieties are delicious for stir-frying or soups. They can be fried and used as a garnish for salads. For frying, there is no need to soak the noodles. They are fried in a dry stage. Be prepared to fish them out of the hot oil immediately as they will puff up like popcorn as soon as they hit the oil. They are ready in a manner of seconds. They will keep for years, stored in a cool, dry place. These noodles are wheat-free, fat-free, cholesterol-free, egg-free and are a healthy option for people with allergies or special nutritional needs. *(Also see, Rice Noodle Preparation, page 201.)*

Rice Noodles, Fresh *(sen yai)*: Made from rice flour and water, and steamed until cooked. These are the same noodles that are commonly sold dried, but are packaged fresh before the drying process. The taste and texture will be slightly different. Since they are fresh, to prevent them from sticking together, the noodles are coated with oil. Fresh rice noodles are soft and, white, resemble sheets of white jello and are often sold in folded sheets. You can cut these sheets into the size noodle you prefer. These noodles are often sold on the counter of Asian markets or in the fresh department wrapped in cellophane. They are delicious for stir-frying or soups. They will dry quickly or become hard in the refrigerator. Place them in warm water to soften them before cooking. Best when used the same day of purchase but will keep in the refrigerator for several days. Wheat-free, gluten-free, cholesterol-free, egg-free.

Rice Paper Wrappers *(pan hoa poi pieh)*: Are paper-thin, semi-transparent, hard rice sheets made of rice flour and water that are used for fresh or fried "eggroll-style" rolls. Commonly used in Vietnamese cuisine for the popular, not fried, spring or shrimp rolls. They come round or in triangular shape. To use these wrappers: just before rolling, individually soak them in a shallow dish with water or place them between two generously damp towels for 30 to 60 seconds to soften, lay them on a flat surface, stuff them with your favorite goodies and roll. Wrappers are made with the same ingredients as dried rice noodles. Since they are steamed-cooked before being dried and packaged, they can be eaten after they are soaked and softened. Most commonly eaten unfried; however, these wrappers can be fried for a light, crispy, smoother roll (not bumpy like egg rolls). Similar to spring roll wrappers but not made with wheat or egg. If you like rolls and don't want the fat from frying, these wrappers are delicious alternatives as you can enjoy 'rolls' without the frying. Since these rolls are commonly referred to as spring rolls in restaurants, ask your server before ordering whether they are fried or not fried. (see also Eggroll Wrappers and Spring Roll Wrappers.)

Rice Stick: (see, Rice Noodles).

Rice Vermicelli: (see, Rice Noodles).

Rice Vinegar (see, Vinegar, Rice).

Roasted Red Chili Paste (nam prik pow): A mild hot and spicy paste made from roasted garlic, shallots and chilies. This paste is commonly used to flavor soups or stir-fry dishes. Just add a tsp. or any desired amount to flavor soups, stir-fries and steamed entrees. Some like to use it as a condiment. The flavor will give your food a smoky, wok-charred flavor. (Also see, Roasted Red Chili Paste, page 195 and Curry Paste, page, 199.)

Sai Fun: (see, Bean Thread Noodles).

Sen Mee: (see, Rice Noodles).

Sesame Oil (num man nga): Made from the pressing of toasted sesame seeds. The color of the oil depends on the color of the toasted seeds. Sesame oil is usually dark amber or a golden copper color. Should not be confused with the clear cold-pressed sesame oil sold in many health food stores. Sesame oil should be used solely as a flavoring agent and not for cooking. Many people often want to stir-fry with this oil when preparing Asian dishes. This is a mistake and will ruin your dinner. This oil is a very thin oil and will char and burn with high heat; leaving your dish with a burnt taste. Use heavier oils such as peanut, corn or soybean for stir-frying. Sesame oil adds a wonderful taste and aroma to your food and should be only drizzled on top of your finished dish just before serving. It is also delicious as a salad dressing oil.

Sesame Paste (gnaa): Toasted white sesame seeds are ground to form a peanut butter-like paste. The flavor is rich and nutty with a definite concentrated sesame flavor. Colors range from brown to golden brown. This paste is used to add a nutty flavor to soups and seasonings. In Middle Eastern food, a similar paste called tahini is made from untoasted white sesame seeds.

Shallots *(hom lek)*: Resembling a small red onion, the flavor gives Thai food a distinct Thai quality. These slender, pear shaped bulbs with long necks and skins can range in color from grey to copper and are more intense in taste than regular onions. They have a mild, sweet, delicate, richer flavor. They are grown in small clusters and are seasonal. They do not keep as well as regular onions and are mostly used for flavoring rather than as a vegetable. Browning shallots will make their taste bitter. A good substitute is the white portion of green onions or, of course, regular onions.

Shrimp *(khung)*: Thailand's Gulf Coast is home to the giant shrimp that are dignified with the name prawns. Large shrimp and prawns are identical; however, varieties from different parts of the world may have different qualities. Tiger prawns are one particular variety often used by name on many menus *(see, Tiger Prawns)*.

Shrimp, Dried *(khung haeng)*: Tiny shrimp are soaked in water and salt, then dried. These bright orange-colored shrimp have a strong shrimp-salt taste and are slightly chewy. The distinct shrimp flavor is often used in soup or stir-fry dishes; it is a flavoring agent in both Thai and Mexican cooking. Typically ground or pounded with other ingredients in a curry paste or sauce, dried shrimp add an intense seafood flavor to food. Usually sold in small packets. Look for brightly colored shrimp; seal and refrigerate leftovers. Available in Asian and Mexican markets. Use in their dry state or soak to soften them for cooking. A small amount will add a lot of flavor.

Shrimp Paste *(kapi)*: Salted fermented shrimp are ground together to form a pungent, strong flavored fish paste that is a pinkish grey color. Some may find the smell of shrimp paste an offensive odor. Before you open a the bottle or package, be prepared for the strong aroma that will soon dominate your kitchen. However, once cooked the smell transforms into a fragrant and aromatic delicious fish and salt taste that is impossible to duplicate. The fresh paste is rose pink and the dried varies in shades of grey/pink/beige. Both are made from ground salted shrimp. The dried, more pungent tasting is dried in the sun so that the moisture is evaporated and the paste is more concentrated. The dried does not need to be refrigerated; however, the fresh should be refrigerated. Rich in vitamin B, it is the main source of protein for most Asian diets.

Siamese Ginger: *(see, Galangal)*.

Soup Rice Noodles: *(see, Rice Noodles)*.

Soy Sauce *(si iu)*: An ancient seasoning first developed in China more than 3,000 years ago. It is a dark brown liquid with a salty taste. Made by fermenting soybeans and mixed with a roasted grain (usually wheat, barley or rice), it is then left in vats for a few months to ferment. The Japanese adopted the process about four centuries after the Chinese. Chinese and Japanese soy sauces have different flavor characteristics and profiles. There are many versions of soy sauce in China with taste profiles that reflect the taste of that particular region. Japanese soy sauce is characteristically sweeter than the Chinese type. However, all soy sauces differ in flavor and color, and vary from light to dark, from thick to watery. Like wine, experiment with different types to find one that suits your taste. Soy sauce is a good substitute for fish sauce when making dish vegetarian.

Spices *(kreung phrong)*: The classic spices associated with Asian and

South Asian cooking actually play a less prominent role in Thai cuisine. Thai curries are usually pastes made from fresh herbs and vegetables as opposed to the Madras curry of India that is a blend of various spices ground into a powder. The recipes in this book call for a number of spices.

Spring Roll Wrappers *(pan hoa poi pieh):* Are thin sheets of wheat, eggs and water. Shapes will vary from round, square or rectangular. Made from the same ingredients as eggroll wrappers, but are much thinner. When fried, they will have a smooth surface, crispy-hard texture. *(Also see, Spring Roll Wrappers and Rice Paper Wrappers.)*

Sticky Rice *(khao niew) / Glutinous Rice, Sweet Rice:* Not as common to the Western table but widely used in Southeast Asian cuisine. In Northern Thailand, sticky rice is steamed and eaten out of hand by scooping up a small portion and slipping it into the curry or other dish, using rice to grasp a piece of meat or vegetable. Sticky rice is also commonly cooked with coconut milk and sugar and served with fruit such as mangoes for dessert or used to make sweet puddings. The short-grained, semi-oval, pearl-shaped, white variety is most common. There is also a black variety that is used only to make desserts. When cooked, sticky rice is soft, moist, sweet, sticky and semi translucent. It is often wrapped up in lotus leaves and stuffed with meat. The Japanese pound cooked glutinous rice to make mochi cakes. This rice is usually steamed not boiled. For best results, soak the grains in water for several hours or overnight; drain all water before cooking. *(Also see, Cooking Sticky Rice, page, 200.)*

Stir-Fry Rice Noodles: *(see, Rice Noodles).*

Sweet Bean Sauce *(see euw):* A rich and full-bodied sauce made from the fermentation of soybeans and sugar. Thais often mix in additional sugar and rice vinegar and add chilies to make a condiment for noodles and appetizers. There are many different consistencies, from a liquid to a paste. Thai sweet bean sauce should not be confused with bean sauces from other Asian countries as they differ in taste.

Sweet Rice: *(see, Sticky Rice).*

Tamarind *(som ma kham piak)*: Tamarind provides the complex fruity and sour taste that is evident throughout Thai cuisine. The flavor is close to sour prunes or a very fruity mild vinegar. It is commonly used in Thai curries, soups and stews. Pods that resemble large peanuts with a hard, smooth and furry brown shell grow on the tamarind tree. The pods are originally green and turn a rich, dark brown color when ripe. Thais eat unripe pods with sugar, salt and chili flakes. They also roast the seeds and use them to flavor young coconut or palm. The pods contain a dark brown, veiny pulp, the consistency of a raisin pulp, surrounding the seeds. The taste of tamarind is most familiar to Western palates as one of the main ingredients in Worcestershire Sauce. Tamarind paste is available from Asian and Indian markets but may be still difficult to find. Tamarind is usually sold in a paste form or as a brick or in jars of concentrated pulp. To use in food, the fleshy pulp must be removed from the fibers and seeds – which is no easy task. When a recipe calls for tamarind, it usually refers to tamarind juice. The juice is used as a souring agent *(see: Tamarind Juice)*. Thais eat tamarind directly from the pod for use as a diuretic. There is no need to worry, tamarind is in a very diluted form when used in food. The taste is impossible to duplicate. Translated from Arabic, tamarind means Indian date. *(Also see, Tamarind Juice/Paste, page 195.)*

Tamarind Juice *(nam som ma kham)*: Concentrated tamarind pulp is sold in small blocks in Asian markets. To use the pulp to make tamarind juice, soak or boil the concentrated pulp in water and use the resulting liquid for cooking. *(Also see, Tamarind Juice/Paste, page 195.)*

Tapioca Pearls *(sa khu met lek)*: Come from the root of the cassava plant. These are very small opaque balls used to thicken sauces as well as puddings and desserts. They become transparent when cooked. *(Also see, Tapioca Starch / Flour)*.

Tapioca Starch / Flour *(Dang Noi or Man Sum Palung)*: Comes from grinding the root of the cassava plant which is native to South America. An off-white colored starch that is also known as tapioca flour or flower, it comes in many textures from fine flour to a small round granular form known as *tapioca pearls.* It is often combined with rice flour or wheat starch to add strength to dough or to thicken sauces. Chefs prefer using tapioca starch to thicken sauces because it is more stable for reheating. Cultivation of the plant in Asia began in the 1800's. The raw root contains toxic portions of hydrocyanic or prussic acid, but once cooked and processed is safe for consumption.

Taro Root *(puak)*: This rough, dark skinned and hairy textured root comes in many sizes, from large melon to small baseball. The meat core will vary in color from white and gray to light purple when cooked. The meat is starchy in texture with a mellow sweet crunchiness. The root is very similar to potatoes in texture and appearance. Taro grows wild in Thailand along river banks and lakes. It is most prevalent in Northern Thailand. The young leaves are also eaten. Taro root is commonly used to give seasonings and sauces texture and a mild sweet flavor.

Thai Holy Basil: *(see, Basil, Thai).*

Thai Lime: *(see, Kaffir Lime).*

Tiger Prawns: *(see, Prawns, Tiger).*

Tofu *(toa hua)*: As more Americans become familiar with it, tofu or bean curd is no longer just a cultural cliché for blandness. Prepared as part of an intensely flavored dish (and Thai food is definitely intensely flavored), its ability to absorb the flavors of what is being cooked make this high-protein and low cholesterol food tasty and healthy. There are many different forms of tofu – puffs, sheets, sticks, blocks. The most common are the white shaped blocks. Tofu blocks come in many different textures – soft, firm, hard, and spongy. Different water densities will determine the texture. Tofu is made from ground soybeans and water, the juice extracted from the meat. The liquid is then cooked and let to stand to form the tofu block. Tofu can be eaten hot or cold. It is often served with sauces that are easily absorbed. Clear white colored tofu is the best. Tofu will keep in the refrigerator for a few days. Discard any tofu that develops a strong odor or changes in color.

Turmeric *(kha-min)*: A small bright orange root that provides the yellow coloring for curries and other dishes. Turmeric is commonly available in powder form. There is also a white version about the same size as common ginger. It has a slightly peppery and pleasant tang. The flowers are used as a vegetable and are stir-fried or steamed.

Vegetables, Preserved/Pickled *(puk dong)*: There are many different varieties of preserved vegetables. Preserved or pickled vegetables usually have a pungent sweet-salty, vinegar taste. Many are pickled with chili for a spicy taste. There are many different ways of preserving vegetables – as you will see in the taste. The most common methods of preserving/pickling use vinegar, salt, water and chilies. These vegetables are used to add a crunch, saltiness, sweetness or a distinct flavor to soups, stir-fries, just about anything you are cooking. They are also served as a side dish with the main course.

Vinegar, Rice *(num som sai choo)*: Usually golden in color, this vinegar has a sweet, light, fuller flavor than regular distilled white vinegar. The taste is quite different from that of regular vinegar, which has a strong acid taste. Compared to vinegars that are usually made by fermenting cider, wine or malt, rice vinegar is made by the fermentation of rice and is less tart and sour. The color is usually clear or slightly golden to light amber. Some rice vinegars contain sugar.

Water Chestnuts *(haew)*: Small round bulbs with papery brown-black skin and a tubular pointy top. Water chestnuts seem more related to a flower bulb than their hard-shelled namesake. Inside is a sweet, slightly starchy flesh. The crunchy flesh of fresh water chestnuts has a sweetness that you just don't get in the canned version. However, both fresh and canned water chestnuts retain their crunchy texture long after they are cooked. Jicama is a good substitute. For some reason, many food writers seem compelled to describe peeling fresh water chestnuts as a fiendishly bothersome task. Not so. Rinse fresh water chestnuts well with water to remove any mud. Slice off the top and bottom and go around the middle with a paring knife. Peel the brown skin off to reveal the white flesh. Cut, chop to your desired taste. Place in a bowl of water to prevent discoloration.

Peeled water chestnuts can be frozen up to a month. Rinse canned water chestnuts under water and blanch them in boiling water to eliminate any can taste or off flavor. Canned water chestnuts should be transferred into a tightly sealed container, filled with water and refrigerated. They will keep up to a week if the water is changed daily. If you're buying them fresh, feel each one and make sure it is firm. Unpeeled they'll keep about two weeks in the refrigerator.

Wide-Style Rice Noodles: *(see, Rice Noodles)*.

Equivalents

Your market may not carry the full line of Thai Kitchen products. Also, some fresh produce native to Asia may be difficult to find in your area. These are not obstacles to your enjoyment of Thai cooking. Simply substitute a few ingredients or you can leave them out to allow the other distinctive herbs to become the main flavor. On the following pages are some ideas. Though they may not be perfect equivalents, they will still give your dish the essence of Thai spirit and flavor.

Curry Paste, Thai Kitchen Green
Substitute Thai Kitchen Red Curry Paste or any Asian or Indian green curry paste. *(Also see, Curry Paste, Green, page 173 and Curry Paste, page 199.)*

To make your own green curry paste: Add 1 Tbs. of oil to a skillet. Sauté together, 3 Tbs. chopped shallots, 1 Tbs. minced garlic and 1 tsp. chopped galangal (or Chinese ginger) for 1 minute until ingredients are fragrant. Remove and add to a blender with 10-15 fresh green chilies (to desired heat level), 1 Tbs. minced lemon grass (or Thai Kitchen Lemon Grass Dried), ½ tsp. chopped kaffir lime leaves, 1 tsp. cilantro root (or cilantro leaves), ½ tsp. pepper, 1 tsp. coriander, 1 tsp. cumin, 1 tsp. salt, 1 tsp. shrimp paste (or whole small Asian dried shrimp). Pulse the blender until all ingredients are mixed well and paste forms. Will store for 3 months in a tightly sealed container in the refrigerator.

Curry Paste, Thai Kitchen Red
Substitute Thai Kitchen Green Curry Paste or any Asian or Indian green curry paste. *(Also see, Curry Paste, Red, page 173 and Curry Paste, page 199.)*

To make your own red curry paste: Add 1 Tbs. of oil to a skillet. Sauté together, 3 Tbs. chopped shallots, 4 Tbs. minced garlic and 1 Tbs. chopped galangal (or Chinese ginger) for 1 minute until ingredients are fragrant. Remove and add to a blender with 10-15 fresh red chilies (to desired heat level), 1 tsp. minced lemon grass (or Thai Kitchen Lemon Grass Dried), ½ tsp. chopped kaffir lime leaves, 1 tsp. cilantro root (or cilantro leaves), ½ tsp. pepper, 1 tsp. coriander, 1 tsp. cumin, 1 tsp. salt, 1 tsp. shrimp paste (or whole small Asian dried shrimp). Pulse the blender until all ingredients are mixed well and paste forms. Will store for 3 months in a tightly sealed container in the refrigerator.

Fish Sauce, Thai Kitchen Premium
Use in place of salt or soy sauce to season almost any savory dish or stir-fry. Although the flavor will not be as robust, you can substitute with soy sauce. (Also see, Fish Sauce, page 174.)

Galangal
Ginger mixed with a little lemon juice can be used as a substitute. *(Also see, Galangal, page 175.)*

Kaffir Lime Leaves
There is no perfect substitute for this unique item. You can substitute lime zest for the citrus taste or use dried Thai sweet basil or even dried bay leaves for a woodsy-leaf flavor. Also try lemon thyme, lemon verbena, bergamot powder, lemon or lime leaves. Since kaffir lime leaves are difficult to find, do not let this keep you from preparing delicious Thai

dishes. They are optional in many of our recipes. You can leave them out and have the other ingredients in your dish convey the unique Thai flavors. (*Also see, Kaffir Lime, page 177.*)

Lemon Grass

Only the moist, juicy bulb-like, white-yellow portions or the bottom few inches of each stalk are used for cooking. Fresh lemon grass may be difficult to find and is optional in many of the recipes except for those in which it is the primary ingredient. Dried lemon grass does not compare to the fresh herb. Since there is no perfect substitute for this unique flavor, leave it out of your dish and allow your other ingredients to convey your Thai flavor. (*Also see, Lemon Grass, pages 178, 199.*) Or, experiment with these alternatives.

- Lemon zest with small amounts of fresh ginger. Approximately ½ Tbs. combination total for 1 lemon grass stalk.

- A few leaves of lemon balm or lemon leaves. Approximately 2 leaves for 1 lemon grass stalk.

- Thai Kitchen Lemon Grass (Dried). Mix 1 Tbs. with ¼ cup of hot water; steep for a few minutes. Strain mixture through a fine sieve or a coffee filter to remove lemon grass particles. The resulting liquid is a lemon grass concentrate. It should be added to your stock at the beginning of the recipe. This portion substitutes for 1 lemon grass stalk.

- Thai Kitchen Tom Yum Hot & Sour Soup Mix. Use 1 tsp. for 1 lemon grass stalk.

Lemon Grass Salad Splash, Thai Kitchen

Combines the delicate aromatic lemon flavor of fresh lemon grass with a handful of authentic Thai spices for a delicious fat free dressing. For a Thai twist, use it in place of vinegar in coleslaw or potato salad. You can substitute Lemon Grass Salad Splash with this blend: 1 Tbs. rice vinegar, 2 Tbs. sugar, 1 Tbs. water, 1 Tbs. fresh lime juice and any chili sauce (to desired spice level).

Light Plum Spring Roll Sauce, Thai Kitchen

A fruity and tangy sauce and dip made with fresh, hand-picked, sweet Thai plums and blended with Thai spices. Substitute with any Asian plum sauce or duck sauce. Or, try apricot jam mixed with a little water, sugar and salt.

Peanut Satay Sauce (Original Recipe or Spicy), Thai Kitchen
A delicious peanut sauce made following a traditional old-fashion Thai recipe. Most commonly used as a dip for satay chicken, this delicious sauce can also be used for stir-frying or in marinades. Fresh peanuts and Thai spices are simmered with the cool sweetness of fresh coconuts to create a savory sauce ideal for grilled or barbecue meats. Substitute with Quick Peanut Satay Sauce recipe on page 114. To make spicy, add a chopped fresh red or green chili to recipe or add more red curry paste.

Red Chili Dipping Sauce, Thai Kitchen
A tangy-sweet & spicy condiment made with fresh, hand-picked, whole Thai chili peppers and spices. Substitute with any Asian sweet chili sauce.

Roasted Red Chili Paste, Thai Kitchen
A concentrated blend of slowly roasted red chilies and authentic Thai spices for a spicy, deep and smoky delicious flavor. Substitute with any Asian spicy bean sauce, spicy soybean paste, a mild chili paste or a spicy bean curd paste. (*Also see, Roasted Red Chili Paste, page 182, and Curry Paste, page 193.*)

To make your own roasted red chili paste: Add 1 Tbs. of oil to a skillet. Sauté together, 8 small sliced shallots and 6 cloves of minced garlic for 1 minute until ingredients are fragrant and golden brown. Remove and add to a blender with ½ - 1 cup whole dried Asian shrimp, ¼ - ½ cup dried red chilies (to desired heat level), and 1 Tbs. sugar. Pulse the blender until all ingredients are mixed well. Add 3 Tbs. fish sauce, 1 ½ Tbs. tamarind juice, 1/3 tsp. salt, and cooled oil from the skillet used to fry the shallots and garlic. Blend until all ingredients are mixed well and a paste forms. Will store for 3 months in a tightly sealed container in the refrigerator.

Spicy Thai Chili Sauce, Thai Kitchen
A delicious hot sauce made from fresh, hand-picked Thai chilies, blended with garlic and Thai spices. It will add flavor and spice, not just heat. Use it in place of hot sauce or ketchup. Substitute with any Asian hot chili sauce or any Asian spicy chili sauce with garlic.

Tamarind Juice/Paste
A good standard proportion is 1 part tamarind pulp concentrate to 8 parts of water. (Example: ¼ cup concentrated tamarind pulp with 2 cups of water). If you like a stronger flavor, reduce the amount of water.

First, boil the concentrated pulp for 5 minutes or soak it in cold water for 1 hour. Work the mixture with your fingertips or spatula until soft, then strain in a strainer or a coffee filter to remove the pulp and extract the liquid. You may want to squeeze the pulp to extract more liquid. It is usually this liquid that you use for recipes. Measure out the amount of liquid in the recipe and refrigerate or freeze the remaining tamarind juice for future use. (For a lighter tamarind juice, you can soak the pulp in more water). You can substitute with Worcestershire; use equal amounts as requested in a recipe. Or, substitute fresh lime juice for the sour taste. Use 1 ½ tsp. of fresh lime juice for 1 tsp. tamarind paste in a recipe. (Also see, Tamarind, page 186.)

Thai Barbecue Sauce, Thai Kitchen
Spices and Thai chilies are combined to create a mildly-spicy, tangy barbecue sauce deliciously different and more flavorful than ordinary American style sauces. Substitute with any American barbecue sauce mixed with vinegar and hot sauce to taste.

Tom Yum Hot & Sour Soup Mix, Thai Kitchen
A concentrated seasoned soup base made from a blend of fresh Thai chilies, lemon grass and authentic Thai herbs and spices. This soothing and warming mixture is Thailand's most basic soup base. There is no perfect substitute for this unique flavor, but you can use a beef, chicken or vegetable bouillon.

To make your own tom yum hot & sour soup paste: In a blender or with a mortar and pestle, blend together 1-2 small dried red chilies (to desired heat level), 1 tsp. salt, 1 ½ tsp. chopped fresh lemon grass (or Thai Kitchen Lemon Grass Dried), 2 medium shallots, 1 tsp. shrimp paste (or whole small Asian dried shrimp) and 1 tsp. vegetable oil. Pulse the blender until all ingredients are mixed well and paste forms. Will store for 3 months in a tightly sealed container in the refrigerator.

Cooking Tips

As part of our mission to take the mystery out of Thai cooking, Thai Kitchen wants to share a few techniques that may be new to you. How do you know how much curry to add? What's an easy way to prepare rice noodles? And, what *do* you do with sticky rice? None of this is baffling when you know how, so read on.

Bamboo Skewers

They should be pre-soaked in water to prevent their burning off during cooking. This is not necessary if they are soaked in the marinade with the meat.

Curry Paste

Since the grinding of fresh ingredients makes curry pastes, the flavor and the heat will naturally vary from season to season, batch to batch and jar to jar. How much curry should you add? It is always a good tip to start with a scant 1 Tbs. of curry paste (or half the recommended amount in a recipe) and adjust to your taste or spice comfort level. (*Also see, Curry Paste, page 173, and Equivalents, page 193.*)

Deep Frying

Deep frying is a challenge and it is made easy by preparing your kitchen in advance. Start by choosing a large (4 quart or bigger) pan. You will also need 2 large slotted serving spoons to remove what you are frying from the oil. Have a large plate (or a cookie sheet) ready with a few layers of absorbent paper towels to place your fried items to drain the excess oil. Do not use olive oil! Plain vegetable oil is the best. It will not impart any flavor to your food. Keep your oil between 325°F and 350°F.

Lemon Grass

To cook with lemon grass, cut off the bottom moist portion of each stalk and discard the fibrous trunks and leaves. This bottom portion of the stalk should be bruised with the back of a knife and then cut or sliced into smaller pieces so that its woodsy/lemon-perfume flavor is easily released during cooking. This is one of the most common flavors used in Thai cooking. Use slices or whole pieces in your cooking. Use lemon grass like a bay leaf or a cinnamon stick to flavor dishes. Finely minced, it can be included in curry pastes and sauces. Since lemon grass is fibrous, and difficult to swallow, remove it from your dish before serving. (*Also see, Lemon Grass, page 178, and Table of Equivalents, page 194.*)

Rice / Preparing and Cooking

How much water to use? We recommend 2 parts of water to 1 part of rice (see below).

Rinsing rice: Start with Thai Kitchen Jasmine Rice. Empty rice into the bowl or pot, hold the utensil under the faucet and start gently running cold water into it. Wash the rice until the water runs clear. You can also use a fine sieve. Drain all excess water before cooking.

Rice Cooker: For the best results, we recommend using a rice cooker. Available in most department stores, and this will be one appliance you will really use. Rinse rice, add suggested amount of water and follow manufacturer's instructions.

Stove Top: If you do not have a rice cooker, you can use a 2 quart saucepan with tight fitting lid. Place rinsed rice in saucepan and add the necessary amount of water. Cook on medium high heat, uncovered, until water begins to boil. Cook until the water has evaporated from the surface or small circles appear on the surface of the rice (about 7 to 10 minutes). Immediately reduce heat to low and cover pan with the lid. Cook for an additional 10 to 15 minutes until rice is tender and all water has evaporated.

Rice Tips: For perfect rice every time, we recommend that once it is cooked, unplug the cooker or remove rice from the heat and allow it to stand covered for an additional 5 minutes. This will allow excess moisture to evaporate and for each rice grain to become more tender and separate. We also recommend not stirring rice while it is cooking. *(Also see glossary, Jasmine Rice, page 179.)*

Uncooked Rice	Water	Cooked Rice
½ cup (4 oz.)	1 cup (8 oz.)	1 ½ cups
1 cup (8 oz.)	2 cups (16 oz.)	3 cups
1 ½ cups (12 oz.)	3 cups (24 oz.)	4 ½ cups
2 cups (16 oz.)	4 cups (32 oz.)	6 cups

Sticky Rice, Cooking
Sticky rice is available in Asian stores and some natural food stores. It needs to be soaked and then steamed in a bamboo steamer lined with cheesecloth or in a steamer insert over a large pot of boiling water. *(Also see, Sticky Rice, page 185.)*

Fried Rice
Leftover rice that has been refrigerated overnight (or longer) produces fantastic fried rice results -- as the rice grains do not stick and clump together during stir-frying. The rice will be slightly hard and probably in

a large clump when removed from the refrigerator. Take the rice and crumble it with your fingers or a spoon into your wok. Add ½ tsp. water (or more) to your wok when stir-frying to soften the rice. Once you taste the delicious results, you will definitely want to save the rice the next time you have Asian take-out.

Rice Noodle Preparation

Traditional Method: Soak dried rice noodles in room temperature water for at least 1 hour or even overnight. Be sure there is enough water to completely immerse the noodles. After 1 hour, they should be soft, firm but flexible. At this point they are ready for cooking. Drain the water before using.

Quick Preparation: Bring enough water to a boil to cover the noodles (or you can use very hot tap water). Turn off heat and immerse rice noodles in hot water for 3-7 minutes until noodles are soft, cooked through but still firm and al dente, not mushy (check firmness frequently, as you would regular pasta). Rinse with cold water for 30 seconds and drain well.

Rice Noodle Tips

After softening noodles with water, they must be kept moist or they will turn hard. If you do not use them immediately, we recommend that you cover the noodles with plastic wrap or a damp cloth.

You can also keep noodles moist by soaking them in water, room temperature or refrigerated, for up to 2 days.

If noodles are not softened completely before cooking, and are still hard while you are stir-frying, add ½ tsp. water (or more) to your skillet. Stir-fry until noodles are soft and water cooks away.

For tastier soup noodles, we recommend using one of the preparation methods mentioned before adding noodles to the soup. Preparing the noodles first, will make them less starchy in your soup, they will not clump and stick together.

(Also see Glossary, Rice Noodles, Dried, page 180.)

Stir-Frying

You do not need a wok to be a stir-fry master. A large skillet will do the trick. The secret to stir-frying is in the preparation. Since this is a quick method of cooking, it is vital to have all your ingredients prepared, chopped, diced or cubed ready next to your cooking area so that you can add them quickly and easily. Choose a wok or skillet large enough to accommodate your ingredients. Place it on high heat. Add 1 to 2 Tbs. vegetable oil. Swirl the oil in the wok to coat the surface. Heat the wok until the oil is hot (but not smoking), about 30 seconds to 1 minute. It is important to have the oil hot before you begin to stir-fry. Now you are ready to begin your recipe.

Move the food around quickly, using a wok shovel or pancake turner to stir, toss, and fold. Do not overcook. Serve hot.

Metric Conversions

Some of the conversions have been rounded for your convenience.

USA

oz. – ounce
lb. – pound
in. – inch
ft. – foot
fl. oz. – fluid ounce
Tbs. – Tablespoon

tsp. - teaspoon
pt. - pint
qt. – quart
gal. – gallon

Metric

g - gram
kg - kilogram
mm – millimeter
cm - centimeter
mL - milliliter
L - liter

Dry Weight

	1 ounce	1 pound	1 milligram	1 gram	1 kilogram
1 ounce	1	1/16	2835	28.35	.028
1 pound	16	1	*	454	.454
1 milligram	1/29,000	*	.1	.001	.000001
1 gram	.032	.002	1000	1	.001
1 kilogram	.000032	2.2	1,000,000	1000	1

	1 pint	1 quart	1 liter
1 pint	1	1/2	.55
1 quart	2	1	1.1
1 liter	1.82	.91	1

1 oz. = 30 g
2 oz. = 60 g
3 oz. = 90 g
4 oz. (¼ lb.) = 125 g
5 oz. (1/3 lb.) = 155 g
6 oz. = 185 g
7 oz. = 220 g

8 oz. (½ lb.) = 250 g
10 oz. = 315 g
12 oz. (¾ lb.) = 375 g
14 oz. = 440 g
16 oz. (1 lb.) = 500 g
1 ½ lbs. = 750 g
2 lbs. = 1 kg

Linear Measures

1 centimeter = 0.394 inch
1 meter = 39.37 inches
1/8 inch = 3 mm
¼ inch = 6 mm
½ inch = 12 mm
1 inch = 2.54 cm
2 inches = 5 cm
3 inches = 7.5 cm
4 inches = 10 cm

5 inches = 13 cm
6 inches = 15 cm
7 inches = 18 cm
8 inches = 20 cm
9 inches = 23 cm
10 inches = 25 cm
11 inches = 28 cm
12 inches / 1 ft. = 30 cm

Fluid Volume Measures

	1 tsp.	1 Tbs.	1 fl. oz.	¼ cup	½ cup	1 cup	1 fl. pt.	1 fl. qt.	1 gal.	1 mL	1 L
1 tsp.	1	1/3	1/16	1/12	1/24	1/48	1/96	1/192	1/768	5	.005
1 Tbs.	3	1	½	¼	1/8	1/16	1/32	1/64	1/256	15	.015
1 fl. oz.	6	2	1	½	¼	1/8	1/16	1/32	1/128	29.56	.030
¼ cup	12	4	2	1	1/2	¼	1/8	1/16	1/64	59.12	.059
½ cup	24	8	4	2	1	½	¼	1/8	1/32	118.2	.118
1 cup	48	16	8	4	2	1	½	¼	1/16	236	.236
1 fl. pt.	96	32	16	8	4	2	1	½	1/8	473	.473
1 fl. qt.	192	64	32	16	8	4	2	1	¼	946	.946
1 gal.	768	256	128	64	32	16	8	4	1	3785	3.785
1 mL	.203	.068	.034	.017	.008	.004	.002	.001	.0003	1	.001
1 L	203	67.68	33.81	16.90	8.453	4.227	2.113	1.057	.264	1000	1

USA	Metric
1 tsp. = 1/3 Tbs.	*
1 Tbs. = 3 tsp.	*
2 Tbs. = 1 fl. oz.	30 mL
4 Tbs. = ¼ cup or 2 fl. oz.	60 mL
8 Tbs. = ½ cup or 4 fl. oz.	125 mL
16 Tbs. = 1 cup or 8 fl. oz. or ½ pint	250 mL
1 ½ cups = 12 fl. oz.	375 mL
2 cups = 1 pint. or 16 fl. oz.	500 mL
1 quart = 2 pints or 4 cups or 32 fl. oz.	1 L
1 gallon = 4 quarts	4 L

Temperature

	Fahrenheit	Celsius / Centigrade
Water Freezes	32°	0°
Water Simmers	115°	46°
Water Boils – Sea Level	212°	100°
Very Low Oven	250°-275°	121°-133°
Low Oven	300°-325°	149°-163°
Moderate Oven	350°-375°	177°-190°
Hot Oven	400°-425°	204°-218°
Very Hot Oven	450°-475°	232°-246°

Index

Notes

Notes

AUTHENTIC THAI CUISINE

Order your products directly from
Thai Kitchen!

http://www.thaikitchen.com

1.800.967.8424 (THAI)

For USA customers only.

Thai Kitchen / Epicurean International, Inc.
229 Castro Street
Oakland, California 94607 USA
PH. 510.268.0209
FAX 510.834.3102

e-mail: info@thaikitchen.com